OECD Capital Market Series

The Swedish Equity Market, Assessment and Policy Recommendations 2026

OECD
BETTER POLICIES FOR BETTER LIVES

Please cite this publication as:
OECD (2026), *The Swedish Equity Market, Assessment and Policy Recommendations 2026*, OECD Capital Market Series, OECD Publishing, Paris, https://doi.org/10.1787/0db1ebf9-en.

ISBN 978-92-64-33585-1 (print)
ISBN 978-92-64-92580-9 (PDF)
ISBN 978-92-64-76328-9 (HTML)

OECD Capital Market Series
ISSN 3006-5801 (online)

Photo credits: Cover © John Nilsson/Getty Images.

Corrigenda to OECD publications may be found at: https://www.oecd.org/en/publications/support/corrigenda.html.

Foreword

This report provides policy recommendations to further strengthen the functioning of the Swedish equity markets. In addition to a detailed empirical analysis, it draws from interviews and consultations with key institutions and market participants.

The empirical mapping contained in the report illustrates the evolution of both the public and private markets over the past two decades. It also examines the ownership structure of Swedish listed companies and the funding choices of the corporate sector more broadly. International comparisons are included throughout the report, with the ambition of putting Swedish developments into a broader European context. This up-to-date mapping is based on an earlier OECD report from 2025 titled *The Swedish Equity Market: Institutional Framework and Trends.*

Detailed descriptions of data sources, selected indicators and the methodology for data collection and analysis are provided in the Annex. The OECD has also conducted fact-finding missions and consultations with market participants, including Nasdaq Stockholm, domestic pension funds, leading legal and financial advisors, as well as a range of other market stakeholders. The report has benefitted greatly from these interviews and consultations, and the team gratefully acknowledges the contributions.

The report has been prepared by the Capital Markets and Financial Institutions Division of the OECD Directorate for Financial and Enterprise Affairs in co-operation with the Swedish Corporate Governance Institute (SCGI). It was authored by Carl Magnus Magnusson and Laura Torelli under the supervision of Alejandra Medina, Head of the Financial Economics Unit, and Serdar Çelik, Head of Division, all from the OECD. From the Swedish Corporate Governance Institute, the authors are Erik Lidman, Professor of Corporate Law, Mats Isaksson, Director, and Jesper Zackrisson, PhD candidate. The report is part of a broader SCGI project on Swedish capital markets, co-financed by the Nasdaq Nordic Foundation and Vinnova.

Table of contents

FIGURES

TABLES

Abbreviations and acronyms

AIM	Alternative Investment Market	ITP	*Industrins och handelns tilläggspension* (Occupational Pension Scheme for Industry and Trade)
AUM	assets under management	MCR	Minimum Capital Requirement
ATP	*allmän tilläggspension* (general supplementary pension)	MiFID II	Markets in Financial Instruments Directive II
CPI	Consumer Price Index	MTF	multilateral trading facility
CPIF	Swedish Consumer Price Index with fixed interest rate	NGM	Nordic Growth Market
DCS	dual-class shares	NL	Netherlands
DE	Germany	Nomad	nominated adviser
DK	Denmark	OECD	Organisation for Economic Co-operation and Development
ECB	European Central Bank	OMXN40	OMNX Nordic 40
ESA 2010	2010 European System of Accounts	PE	private equity
ESMA	European Securities and Market Authority	PPP	purchasing power parity
ETF	exchange traded fund	PTK	Council for Negotiation and Cooperation
EU	European Union	SCR	Solvency Capital Requirement
EUR	Euro	SE	Sweden
FDI	Foreign Direct Investment	SEB	*Skandinaviska Enskilda Banken*
FoF	fund of funds	SEK	Swedish Krona
FR	France	SIXRX	SIX Return Index
FSA	*Finansinspektionen* (Swedish Financial Supervisory Authority)	SME	small and medium-sized enterprise
GDP	gross domestic product	SPO	secondary public offering (follow-on offering)
IBA	income base amounts	UK	United Kingdom
IFRS	International Financing Reporting Standards	US	United States
INFE	International Network on Financial Education	USD	United States Dollar
IPO	initial public offering	VC	venture capital
IPS	*Individuellt pensionssparande* (individual pension savings)		
ISK	*Investeringssparkonto* (investment savings account)		

Executive summary

The Swedish equity markets, which are among the largest in the European Union (EU) even in absolute terms, have increasingly become a reference point in policy discussions around capital market development, serving as a case study illustrating the approaches that can help promote successful domestic markets. Previous OECD work has highlighted a set of specific policy themes and initiatives, common to consecutive governments, as key drivers of Swedish market dynamism. A changing structure of domestic as well as global markets, however, requires monitoring and, where appropriate, reforms to ensure the continuation of this success. That includes identifying and implementing reforms where changing conditions call for it, but also recognising and safeguarding the underlying policies that have been foundational to market success.

Chapter 1 contains an assessment of recent developments that may merit policy change and specific recommendations to continue strengthening the Swedish market. Chapter 2 provides an empirical mapping of the market, including peer country comparisons.

Summary of policy recommendations

The main policy recommendations are split into six different areas:

- **MTF-listed companies**. Extend the regulated market obligation to disclose acquisitions or disposals of major shareholdings to also cover transactions in companies with shares listed on an MTF. Extend the current takeover sanction regime to include breaches of the MTF Takeover Rules in addition to those on the regulated market. Consider the establishment of a council or working group with the specific purpose of representing the perspective of MTF-listed companies in discussions with other market stakeholders.
- **Takeovers**. Undertake a review of the legal process following a squeeze-out, with the aim of reducing the time required for the procedure following a takeover bid. Any considerations with respect to the threshold for mandatory bids should be based on an analysis of the effectiveness of the current threshold and the costs and benefits of potential changes.
- **Foreign direct investment screening.** Without prejudice to the legitimate screening of foreign investments for national security interests, undertake a review of the FDI Act with a view to reducing its negative effects on the equity market and reducing costs for both public authorities and companies.
- **Directed share issues.** Review and revise the law implementing a supermajority requirement for directed share issues to board members, executives and employees to bring it in line with the threshold for other directed share issues.
- **Dialogue with the Financial Services Authority**. Initiate a consultation with stakeholders, undertake further analysis and, subject to the findings as well as future developments, consider a revision of the supervisory mandate concerning the authorised balance between supervision and guidance.

- **Fund market concentration.** Continue to monitor developments in fund market concentration and seek to identify possible policy levers to promote competition and diversity in the fund market.

Areas to safeguard and monitor

There are many areas of the Swedish equity market that function well and that are the result of focused, long-term policy efforts. To ensure the continuation of these policies in a context of a changing economic, financial and political climate globally, it is worth emphasising certain policy areas that have been particularly important to the Swedish equity market success.

- **Empowering shareholder engagement.** Recognise the importance of the tradition of active ownership engagement by Swedish investors and monitor the effects of the increasing prevalence of passive investment in this respect.
- **Investor protection and minority shareholder rights.** Safeguard the benefits stemming from the well-established system of investor protection in Sweden and ensure potential changes to the legal and regulatory framework are made in close consultation with market stakeholders.
- **Regulatory design.** Recognise and safeguard the merits of the current regulatory framework. Carefully evaluate the costs of any potential changes to the system.
- **Investor heterogeneity.** Monitor structural changes to the investor base that might reduce heterogeneity benefits, such as excessive market concentration, and include investor diversity as a metric when evaluating policy options.

Summary of empirical findings

Public equity markets. Sweden's public equity markets have the highest number of listed companies in the EU. Total market capitalisation amounts to 194% of GDP, clearly surpassing major peer countries. A key characteristic is the substantial activity by smaller companies. Most public companies in Sweden are listed on a growth market (although these segments have seen net delistings since 2023). The median IPO size since 2000 of USD 9 million is much lower than in peer countries. The growth segments work as a stepping stone to the regulated markets: since 2013, an annual average of 45% of new listings on Sweden's regulated markets have originated from a local growth market. Returns on the domestic market have been among the strongest in the world; the main broad local market index has consistently outperformed major international indices over long periods of time, including in foreign currency terms.

Private equity markets. Fundraising by Swedish private equity funds has made up nearly a tenth of the European total in recent years, more than three times what its GDP share would suggest. Nearly two-thirds of total fundraising has come from non-European investors, by far the highest share among peer countries in the EU. Swedish companies are also overrepresented as investment targets, having received 60% more private equity investment than economic weight would suggest between 2019 and 2024. Importantly, there is a strong link between the private and public equity markets: uniquely among peer countries, one of the most common ways for private equity firms to divest their holdings of Swedish companies in recent years has been to take them public.

Institutional investors and ownership. The institutional investor base in Sweden is both sizeable and uniquely exposed to the domestic equity markets. The three main public pension buffer funds (AP2-4), managing aggregate assets of more than EUR 200 billion, have an average equity exposure of 51% of total investment assets, of which roughly 28% is domestic equities. The even larger occupational pension fund sector, with total investment assets of more than EUR 285 billion, also allocates about half of its aggregate portfolio to equities, as does the insurance sector. Investment funds had an aggregate market value of EUR 817 billion at the end of 2025, of which EUR 570 billion was direct equity holdings. Sweden also has a long history of family ownership through investment firms. The five largest family-owned investment firms collectively hold over 8% of total domestic market capitalisation, with stakes in major listed companies. They are heavily involved in local equity markets, taking an active ownership role.

Household investment. Swedish households have among the highest levels of participation in capital markets in Europe, with 10% of total financial assets allocated to investment funds and 7% to listed equities. Only 12% is held in traditional currency and deposits – the lowest among peer countries. While direct equity holdings among Swedish households have declined in recent years, there has been a substantial parallel increase in indirect equity investments through funds.

1 Policy recommendations

This chapter provides policy recommendations to further strengthen the Swedish equity markets, drawing both from in-depth interviews with market participants and the empirical analysis in chapter 2.

1.1. Introduction

In a context where the number of listed companies is decreasing in most advanced economies, the Swedish equity market has generated significant interest among both policymakers and market participants in recent years. As previous OECD work (2025[1]) has highlighted, the market is one of the most dynamic in Europe. It has the highest number of publicly listed companies in the EU in absolute terms and among the highest total market capitalisations, despite being the bloc's ninth largest economy. The growth market segments in particular are very active. Investor returns over the last two decades have been some of the highest in the world. Retail engagement in domestic markets is extensive. The private equity markets are also far larger than economic weight alone would suggest. In addition, Sweden ranks highly in several indices measuring market and corporate sustainability as well as innovation (Block et al., 2024[2]; WIPO, 2023[3]; SolAbility, 2025[4]; Robeco, 2024[5]).

Notably, there does not appear to be any trade-offs between the growth of different types of funding in the Swedish market, which is sometimes proposed as an explanation for the broader advanced economy trend of a declining use of public equity markets, notably the growth of private equity. On the contrary, Swedish private equity funds raised nearly a tenth of all European private equity capital in the last decade, and Swedish companies are overrepresented as investment targets, having received 60% more private equity investment between 2014 and 2024 than the size of the economy would suggest. There is also a strong link between the private and public equity markets. Uniquely among peer countries, one of the most common ways for private equity firms to divest their holdings of Swedish companies in recent years has been to take them public (see sections 2.1.6 and 2.2). As shown in previous OECD work on the Swedish corporate bond market (2022[6]; 2024[7]), in parallel to the past two decades of public and private equity market growth, there has also been strong growth in the corporate bond market.

This dynamism is the result of long-term policy efforts to promote capital market development – supported and guided by a tradition of strong political focus on capital formation, business dynamics, shareholder rights and investor protection – involving several areas that go beyond capital market policy in a narrow sense. As such, as global markets and conditions change, domestic policy will need to respond to ensure the continued success of the Swedish market. This report formulates policy recommendations to that effect, drawing on extensive interviews with local market participants as well as the comprehensive empirical mapping undertaken in previous work and which has been further developed for this report (OECD, 2025[1]). In addition to specific policy recommendations, it seeks to underline areas that have been particularly important to Swedish market development and that are therefore critical to safeguard. These may also be of relevance to broader European initiatives such as the EU's Savings and Investments Union agenda. The recommendations are summarised below.

Table 1.1. Summary of policy recommendations

Policy area	Recommendation
MTF-listed companies	Extend the regulated market obligation to disclose major changes in shareholdings to also cover transactions in companies with shares listed on an MTF.
	Extend the current takeover sanction regime to include breaches of the MTF Takeover Rules in addition to those on the regulated market.
	Consider the establishment of a council or working group with the specific purpose of representing the perspective of MTF-listed companies in discussions with other market stakeholders.
Takeovers	Undertake a review of the legal process following a squeeze-out, with the aim of reducing the time required for the procedure following a takeover bid.
	Any considerations with respect to the threshold for mandatory bids should be based on an analysis of the effectiveness of the current threshold and the costs and benefits of potential changes.
Foreign direct investment	Without prejudice to the legitimate screening of foreign investments for national security interests, undertake a review of the FDI Screening Act with a view to reducing its negative effects on the equity market and reducing costs for both public authorities and companies.

Policy area	Recommendation
Directed share issues	Review and revise the law implementing a supermajority requirement for directed share issues to board members, executives and employees to bring it in line with the threshold for other directed share issues.
Dialogue with the FSA	Examine whether a revision of the FSA's mandate with respect to the balance between supervision and guidance is merited to address concerns raised by market participants regarding the need for further guidance.
Fund market concentration	Monitor concentration levels in the investment fund market and seek to identify policy levers to promote competition and diversity.

Areas to safeguard and monitor

Policy area	Recommendation
Empowering shareholder engagement	Recognise the importance of the tradition of active ownership engagement by Swedish investors and monitor the effects of the increasing prevalence of passive investment in this respect.
Investor protection	Safeguard the benefits stemming from the well-established system of investor protection in Sweden and ensure potential changes to the legal and regulatory framework are made in close consultation with market stakeholders.
Regulatory design	Maintain the current framework of self-regulation/delegated regulation and carefully evaluate the costs of potential changes to the system.
Investor heterogeneity	Monitor structural changes to the investor base that might reduce the benefits from heterogeneity, such as excessive market concentration, and include investor heterogeneity as a metric when evaluating policy options.

1.2. Policy recommendations

1.2.1. The MTF segment

The multilateral trading facility (MTF), or growth market, segment has been an important driver of broader Swedish equity market development. The Swedish MTF market is the largest in the EU, both in terms of the number of listed companies and total market capitalisation, with 551 companies listed across three different MTFs at the end of 2025 – 61% of the total number of domestically listed companies. That is 1.6 times more than the EU's second largest MTF market by number of listed companies (Poland, which had 353 listed companies at the end of 2025, representing 48% of domestically listed firms). In France – the third largest market by number of listed companies and second by market capitalisation – 345 companies were listed at the end of 2025, accounting for 54% of domestic listings. During the past decade, approximately four out of every five new listings in Sweden have been on an MTF. Importantly, these listings often serve as a stepping stone to the regulated markets. Since 2013, an average of 45% of new listings on Swedish regulated markets annually have been companies that were already listed on a local growth market (see Figure 2.13).

There are, however, certain aspects of Swedish policy with respect to MTFs that could usefully be addressed, especially considering the success of the existing Swedish approach of limited regulatory differentiation between MTFs and regulated markets (see section 1.3.2).

Disclosure of acquisition or disposal of major shareholdings

One way in which Swedish regulation differentiates between MTFs and regulated markets relates to the requirement to disclose acquisitions or disposals of major shareholdings. In accordance with the EU Transparency Directive, the Swedish Act on Trading in Financial Instruments (1991[8]) mandates that any shareholder passing key ownership thresholds (5%, 10%, 15%, 20%, 25%, 30%, 50%, 66,66% and 90%) in a company with shares listed on a regulated market must disclose it publicly (so-called "flagging"). This obligation does not, however, apply to transactions in shares of companies listed on MTFs.

The original Swedish rules regarding disclosure of changes in shareholdings, established in 1983, were applicable to all market segments and became limited to regulated markets only with implementation of the EU Transparency Directive in 2004. At that point in time, the number of companies listed on MTFs was very small. Since then, however, as mentioned above and further detailed in section 2.1.6, they have grown to become a very substantial part of the domestic market. With this development in mind, **it is recommended to extend the obligation to disclose major changes in shareholdings to also cover transactions in companies with shares listed on an MTF.** A corresponding extension of the rules was made in Finland in 2024.

Sanctions and takeover rules

The Swedish takeover regulation consists partially of statutory law and partially of self-regulation. Certain fundamental rules (primarily related to the implementation of the EU Takeover Directive) are provided in the Swedish Takeover Act (2006[9]), while most detailed rules are found in the takeover rules issued by the Swedish Stock Market Regulation Committee and adopted by the stock exchanges. The takeover rules become legally binding for an offeror through a section in the Swedish Takeover Act which stipulates that a public takeover bid for shares listed on a regulated market may only be made by an offeror who has made an undertaking to the stock exchange operating the regulated market on which the company's shares are traded. The offeror undertakes to comply with the rules laid down by the stock exchange for such offers, and to submit to the sanctions that the stock exchange may decide upon in the event of a breach of these rules. This undertaking means ensuring compliance with the takeover rules laid down by the exchange, and submitting to the sanctions that the stock exchange may decide upon in the event of a breach thereof. Because the legislative basis for the Swedish takeover rules is the EU Takeover Directive, this does not apply to bids for shares in a company listed on an MTF.

The EU Takeover Directive dates from 2004, at which point the Swedish MTF market was significantly smaller, with very limited takeover activity. Similarly to the dynamics discussed above regarding disclosure of changes in shareholdings, the limitation of the Takeover Act and its sanctions to regulated markets simply reflected the underlying scope of the implemented EU directive, and for twenty years there were no breaches of the Takeover Rules for MTFs despite the lack of binding sanctions. As the MTF segment has grown, however, the number of takeover bids has increased substantially. Between 2020 and 2025, MTF companies were the targets of approximately 70% of all takeover bids in Sweden. In 2025, for the first time since the inception of the Swedish takeover regulation, there were also two cases of offerors not complying with the MTF Takeover Rules, creating uncertainty in the market. Given these developments, and the growing prominence of the Swedish MTF markets since the implementation of the Takeover Act in 2006, **it is recommended to extend the sanction regime to include breaches of the MTF Takeover Rules.**

Fostering dialogue between MTF issuers and other market stakeholders

Several market participants consulted by the OECD have highlighted the culture of and infrastructure for continuous high-level dialogue between key stakeholders from different parts of the Swedish market as fundamental to its success. Co-operation and dialogue between for example the Swedish Association for Institutional Investors (*Institutionella Ägares Förening*) and major domestic investment companies on the investor side, and the Confederation of Swedish Enterprise on the corporate side, allow for sharing of perspectives and the identification of measures that can help improve market functioning. However, while this infrastructure is well-established for large companies listed on regulated markets – both through individual company engagement and the Confederation of Swedish Enterprise – there is no organisation similarly representing firms listed on MTFs. This reflects both the relatively recent development of the MTF segment and the lack of resources to engage in policy debate in a structured manner among smaller companies. There are examples in other jurisdictions of bodies designed for such purposes, such as the Quoted Companies Alliance in the United Kingdom. The lack of such a body risks MTF companies' perspectives not being reflected in policy debates. **It is therefore recommended to consider the establishment of a council or working group with the specific purpose of representing the perspective of companies listed on an MTF.**

1.2.2. Takeovers

The Swedish takeover market is active, with an average of 26 bids per year from 2020-2025. That is similar to the activity in much larger countries like Germany, and significantly higher than peer countries like Denmark, Finland and the Netherlands.[1] One driver of this level of activity is a well-functioning regulatory framework supported by the Swedish Securities Council (*Aktiemarknadsnämnden*) to which the Swedish Financial Supervisory Authority (*Finansinspektionen*, FSA) has delegated the right to issue rulings on public takeover bids. This is reflected in the fact that there were no court cases related to takeover bids in Sweden between 2010 and 2025, as well as the comparatively low costs and short timeframe for carrying out a takeover bid. Estimations by five of Sweden's largest legal advisors solicited for this report suggest an average cost of around USD 2-3 million and a timeframe of approximately 10 weeks (non-competing cash offer without legal complications such as competition law reviews).[2] Even so, stakeholder consultations have helped identify certain areas that merit policy consideration.

Squeeze-outs

Following a takeover bid where the offeror has reached a holding of over 90% of the shares in the target company, a squeeze-out procedure is implemented in accordance with the Swedish Companies Act (2005[10]). Since the procedure is tried by an arbitration tribunal, public data concerning such procedures are not readily available. However, an analysis of a sample of 34 arbitration awards announced between 2020 and 2025 done for this report suggests the average total time for a redemption procedure is 15 months (with advance access, i.e. technical transfer, of the shares taking on average around 4 months). While the length of the procedures varies significantly from case to case, internationally active market participants have noted the procedure is generally lengthy, which can significantly delay restructurings through a takeover process. **An overview of the squeeze-out regime should therefore be undertaken, with the aim of reducing the time required for the procedure following a takeover bid.**

Mandatory bids

Implemented on the basis of the EU Takeover Directive, the current Swedish mandatory bid rule has been in effect since 2006 and stipulates that an owner that reaches 30% or more of the votes in a company listed on a regulated market has to make a public offer for the remaining shares. During consultations with the OECD, some respondents have suggested a review of the threshold for a mandatory bid, while others have expressed satisfaction with the current threshold. **Any further considerations with respect to an appropriate threshold for a mandatory bid should be based on additional analysis of the effectiveness of the current system and the costs and benefits associated with potential changes thereto.**

1.2.3. Foreign direct investment screening

Recent years have seen a global trend towards the introduction or reform of foreign investment related policy with a view to safeguarding security interests (OECD, 2025[11]). Sweden is no exception to this trend. The Swedish Foreign Direct Investment (FDI) Screening Act (2023[12]) was introduced in December 2023. The scope of reporting mandates by the legislation was intentionally set wide to capture all potential sensitive transactions and therefore includes all types of investors, including domestic ones, and a wide range of sectors. This scope is notably wider than those applicable in comparable jurisdictions. In 2024, the first full year in which the rules were in force, there were 1 261 applications under the FDI Screening

Act. That is similar to the total number of applications across Belgium, Finland, France, Germany, the Netherlands and Spain during the same period and nearly six times the average in these countries (Implementeringsrådet, 2026[13]). Between December 2023 and the end of 2025 there were 3 362 applications in Sweden. Of the 3 067 applications for which a decision is available, 97% were unconditionally granted and 0.1% resulted in prohibition of the investment (Inspectorate of Strategic Products, 2026[14]).

Several stakeholders consulted by the OECD have suggested that the regulation does not sufficiently account for the implications on business and equity market functioning. The Swedish government's Implementation Council (2026[13]) has also recommended amendments to the rules, notably with respect to predictability and compliance costs, making reference to the structure of the equity market. The current legislation introduces long delays to what were previously standard transactions, such as intra-group transactions in fully domestic company groups, investments by Swedish investment funds in Swedish companies, and secondary public offerings (SPOs). Given that equity market transactions are often time sensitive, this can create substantial frictions in the market. **Without prejudice to the legitimate screening of foreign investments for national security interests, a review of the FDI Screening Act is recommended, with a view to improving efficiency and reducing cost for both public authorities and companies**. One possible solution to the issues faced by investors and businesses that would not prejudice national security interests may be to introduce the possibility of investors getting an *ex ante* screening, granting them a general dispensation to carry out investments without further screenings conditional on there being no changes in ownership or control in the applicant.

1.2.4. Directed share issues to board members, executives and employees

The Swedish regulatory model includes strong statutory pre-emption rights for existing shareholders. When shares are privately placed without adhering to these pre-emptive rights, these must be approved by the general meeting of shareholders by a two-thirds majority of votes cast and shares represented. For directed issues of shares or warrants to board members, the CEO and other employees of the company, the approval threshold increases to nine-tenths of the general meeting (The Swedish Companies Act, 2005[10]). This supermajority requirement was implemented in the wake of a corporate scandal in the 1980s in which corporate executives received disproportionate allocations in a rights issue on very favourable conditions.

Several stakeholders have noted that the supermajority requirement can create frictions since directed share issues of this character are an important tool in incentive and remuneration programmes, helping attract managerial, board and employee talent, as well as to ensure alignment between managerial and shareholder interests. These frictions have increased in parallel with the growing prevalence of foreign investors in the Swedish market, which represented over a third of identified owners at the end of 2025 (see Figure 2.27), and in particular in a context of increasing passive investment. This is because many passive investors take a standardised approach to voting or abstain from voting altogether on non-standard issues. Since the supermajority requirement is unique to Sweden, increased levels of foreign and passive ownership have complicated the implementation of share-based incentive programmes. In addition, stakeholders have noted the proliferation of market practices where such programmes are designed to avoid requiring a supermajority vote, which both decreases the actual shareholder influence in these matters and makes the programmes unnecessarily costly for companies and shareholders. The supermajority requirement's effect on minority shareholder protection is taken to be small. **With these issues in mind, it is recommended to review and revise the law implementing a supermajority requirement for directed share issues to board members, executives and employees to bring it in line with the threshold for other directed share issues.**

1.2.5. Dialogue with the Financial Services Authority

Stakeholders consider the dialogue with the Swedish FSA (*Finansinspektionen*) to be functioning well in many areas. Issuers and advisors have, however, noted that the nature of the dialogue has changed during the last decade, particularly in areas characterised by complex and principles-based regulation such as the Market Abuse Regulation, reducing legal certainty. Given the inherent interpretative challenges associated with such regulations, market participants have expressed a need for further guidance on the practical application of certain rules. This discussion is ongoing, and the Swedish FSA has indicated an openness to continued engagement with market participants within the framework of its supervisory mandate. Since autumn 2025, the authority has also started taking measures to further strengthen dialogue, including increasing the number of roundtable discussions with stakeholders and issuing additional public guidance. To address the concerns raised by market participants, **the government is recommended to consult with stakeholders, undertake further analysis and, subject to the findings as well as future developments, consider a revision of the supervisory mandate concerning the authorised balance between supervision and guidance.**

1.2.6. Fund market concentration

The Swedish investment fund market has seen an increase in concentration in recent years. This is partly a positive development – given the significant economies of scale inherent in this market segment, consolidation can have benefits in the form of lower management fees for investors. However, it is important to ensure that this does not come at the expense of investor diversity more broadly. Some market participants have raised concerns in this regard. At the end of 2025, the ten largest domestic investment funds held 3.7% of total domestic equity market capitalisation and 31% of total domestic equity assets held by funds (up from 3.3% and 29% in 2019).[3] This coincides with a period of mergers in the market, both in the public pension system through the restructuring of the buffer funds (see Box 2.5) and in the private fund market, in addition to the reform of the Swedish Fund Selection Agency's (*Fondtorgsnämnden*) procurement process. Several stakeholders raised this as a possible concern given the role investment funds play as anchor investors in small and mid-cap companies, since larger fund sizes would bring about corresponding increases in the minimum ticket size, making such investments less viable. Given the role of smaller companies in the success of the Swedish market, **this development merits monitoring and calls for further investigation, including identification of possible policy levers to promote competition and diversity in the fund market.**

1.3. Areas to safeguard and monitor

As noted in previous OECD work (2025[1]), there are many areas of the Swedish equity market that function well and that have contributed to domestic market success, notably a widespread equity culture, a substantial domestic institutional investor base, significant household engagement in local markets, the fluidity of movement between private, growth and regulated public markets, the regulatory design and corporate governance framework. These are all results of focused, long-term policy efforts. In a context of a changing economic, financial and political climate globally, it is worth emphasising certain policy areas that have been particularly important to the Swedish equity market success, with a view to ensuring the continuation of these policies.

1.3.1. Empowering shareholder engagement

The OECD (2025[1]) assessment report of the Swedish equity market noted the domestic corporate governance model as an important driver of the market's development. A distinguishing feature is the clear focus on shareholder control. Swedish company law places control firmly with the shareholders and there are virtually no matters on which the general meeting cannot make binding resolutions or give the board and management directions with respect to, including immediate dismissal. This leaves very limited room for managerial entrenchment. A notable mechanism is the nomination and appointment process for the board of directors. The Swedish Corporate Governance Code stipulates that board member nominees be proposed by a nomination committee, comprising major shareholders or their representatives, that is appointed by the shareholders at the general meeting. This contrasts with practices in many other countries, where nomination committees are usually formed as subcommittees of the board. This shareholder-centric framework is accompanied by an extensive set of rules concerning equal treatment of shareholders, individual shareholder rights and specific minority shareholder rights (Lekvall, 2014[15]; Gilson, 2014[16]; Nenova, 2003[17]).

The model presupposes and encourages active engagement from company shareholders, the culture of which is widespread in Sweden, with controlling as well as minority shareholders often playing an important role. Controlling shareholder engagement is facilitated by the availability and widespread use of dual class share structures, which allows both entrepreneurs and external shareholders with the capacity for engagement to hold a significant proportion of the votes in a company at a lower cost than what otherwise would be possible, and limiting negative free float effects. The Swedish market also features a number of significant family-controlled investment firms and foundations that have large and sometimes controlling stakes in a diverse range of major companies across different sectors of the economy (see Table 2.2).

Other institutional investors, too, are often highly engaged. Pension fund representatives, for example, have noted that their participation in nomination committees and the possibility of actively influencing the general governance of their portfolio companies shape their assessment of investment risk, enabling higher allocations to domestic equities. Notably, Swedish institutional investors have formed an association (*Institutionella Ägares Förening*) with the explicit purpose of facilitating engagement in regulatory matters and system development.

The importance of active ownership engagement in corporate governance issues by Swedish investors should be recognised, and the effects of the increasing prevalence of passive investment in this respect should be monitored.

1.3.2. Investor protection and minority shareholder rights

One of the prevailing narratives seeking to explain the lack of new equity market listings in many jurisdictions relates to excessive regulatory burdens placed on listed companies (see for instance Pagano, Panetta and Zingales (1998[18]); Gao, Ritter and Zhu (2013[19]); Djankov et al (2002[20])). Consequently, deregulatory agendas have gained ground, notably in Europe. While the identification of excessively onerous and possibly duplicative regulation is a legitimate exercise and, if done right, serves to reduce deadweight cost and increase market efficiency, it is imperative to distinguish the regulations that are overly stringent to the detriment of the market from those that are stringent to the ultimate benefit of the market.

One critical area in this regard is investor protection, where Sweden serves as a useful example. A distinct feature of the Swedish regulatory framework is a rigorous regime of shareholder rights and investor protection, with far-reaching regulation concerning equal treatment of shareholders, transparency, strict majority voting requirements and pre-emptive rights, strict rules for related party transactions and specific minority powers including for example the right to demand a second "minority" auditor at the expense of the company, the right to demand extraordinary general meetings to be held and the right to demand minimum dividends to be paid out (Lidman and Skog, 2021[21]).

Several stakeholders, both investors and issuers, have raised the strong investor protection regime in Sweden as a fundamental condition for the market's growth and dynamism, underpinning market trust and attracting investors with different risk profiles. This contributes to lowering the cost of equity capital, enhancing the appeal of listing and allows not just large but also small and early-stage firms to turn to the equity market for financing.

This is also visible in the Swedish approach to regulation on MTF markets. In many jurisdictions, the requirements on companies listed on an MTF are significantly less stringent than those applicable on regulated markets. This is reflected in EU law, where many directives, regulations and specific rules apply to companies listed on regulated markets but not on MTFs. Swedish regulation, however, in many areas does not significantly distinguish between companies listed on different venues, generally extending the scope of EU law applicable to companies listed on regulated markets to MTF listings as well (notable exceptions are those discussed in section 1.2.1). This includes, for example, core material regulation on takeovers, related party transactions, share issuance and say on pay. While imposing greater compliance requirements on smaller companies, this may also give investors greater familiarity and certainty with respect to their legal protection on different markets, possibly increasing interest in MTF investments and at the same time make the move from an MTF to a regulated market less imposing from a company perspective. This focus on investor protection has been cited by stakeholders as an important aspect of Swedish MTF market success.

Given the widespread recognition among market participants of the importance of rigorous investor protection in Sweden, **potential changes to the legal and regulatory framework should be made in close consultation with market stakeholders and seek to safeguard the benefits stemming from the well-established system of investor protection**.

1.3.3. Regulatory design and delegated regulation

One of the core functions of capital market regulation is to provide legal clarity and predictability to shareholders and companies, reducing the cost of investing and the cost of capital. A prerequisite for this is not only clear regulation, but also continuous dialogue with supervisory authorities concerning appropriate courses of action and the possibility of binding advance rulings. The latter is a distinguishing feature of the Swedish equity market, most notably through consultations and rulings of the Swedish Securities Council (*Aktiemarknadsnämnden*). As noted in previous OECD (2025[1]) work, Swedish capital market law has a unique structure that puts it somewhere in between a common and civil law system. While the Companies Act provides a general framework and set of rules, the detailed rules governing Swedish equity markets are not laid out in legislation but are instead delegated to a number of bodies such as the Swedish Securities Council, the Stock Market Regulation Committee (*Aktiemarknadens självregleringskommitté*) and the Corporate Governance Board (*Kollegiet för svensk bolagsstyrning*). These bodies are funded by key market actors and have been established in co-operation with the legislator, meaning they have statutory mandates that can make their rulings legally binding.

The Securities Council can issue statements on almost all actions by a listed company or a shareholder in such a company, including matters concerning interpretation of and dispensation from the takeover regulation, the rules concerning directed share issues, the Swedish corporate governance code, incentive programmes and de-listings (though notably not issues concerning prospectuses and the market abuse regulation, which fall under the responsibility of the FSA). Market participants have continuous access to consultations with the Securities Council secretariat, and a formal, binding ruling of the Council can be obtained within two weeks. The Securities Council issues around 60 rulings per year, most of which are made public, contributing to predictability.

Market participants note that this structure provides Swedish equity market regulation with flexibility and rapidity, allowing it to move in step with market developments, as well as giving the market access to cost efficient and rapid dispute resolution. This is part of the reason Sweden has been able to combine a strict investor protection regime with significant market dynamism. As with investor protection, **Swedish**

policymakers should recognise and safeguard the merits of the current regulatory framework. The costs of any potential changes to the system should be carefully evaluated.

1.3.4. Investor heterogeneity

The Swedish market is characterised by a broad investor base of heterogenous actors with respect to risk profiles, investment horizons and engagement strategies, spanning millions of retail investors, a diverse group of domestic institutional investors and professional controlling shareholders. This is, to an extent, the effect of conscious policy decisions. The level of retail investment, for example – with more than one in every three Swedes having a dedicated investment savings account (ISK) – is the result of continuous policy efforts since at least the 1970s. These have included fiscal incentives, but some of the most effective policies, such as the 2012 ISK account, owe their success as much to simplification and lowering access barriers as they do to tax incentives. This is an important policy lesson, highlighting the possibility of stimulating household engagement even without direct fiscal benefits. Policies more indirectly related to capital markets, notably digitalisation of government services and extensive social security coverage, have likely also helped stimulate retail investment activity.

The significance of the institutional investor base, notably pension funds, is also a direct effect of dedicated government policy. Swedish pension fund assets represent more than a fifth of the EU's total, with substantial allocations to domestic equities. This follows from the design of the Swedish pension system, which has had an asset-backed component (through the public buffer funds) since the 1960s, and exposure to equity markets for more than fifty years. Reforms in the 1990s that moved towards a defined contribution system substantially accelerated the importance of the system to domestic capital markets. The public pension system was designed with investor heterogeneity in mind, with management split into several independent funds. Extensive occupational pension fund coverage – 90% of Swedish employees are automatically covered – has also been a major contributing factor to the close connection between pension funds and capital market development. Chapter 2 and OECD (2025[1]) provide further detail on the Swedish investor base and the policies that have helped foster investor heterogeneity.

This diverse investor structure helps promote efficient price discovery, liquidity, and counter-cyclicality, making it a key aspect of the market. **It is therefore important to monitor structural changes to the investor base that might reduce the benefits from heterogeneity, such as excessive market concentration, and to include investor heterogeneity as a metric when evaluating policy options.**

References

Block, S. et al. (2024), *2024 Environmental Performance Index*, Yale Center for Environmental Law & Policy, http://epi.yale.edu. [2]

Djankov, S. et al. (2002), "The Regulation of Entry", *The Quarterly Journal of Economics*, Vol. 117/1, pp. 1-37, https://doi.org/10.1162/003355302753399436. [20]

Gao, X., J. Ritter and Z. Zhu (2013), "Where Have All the IPOs Gone?", *Journal of Financial and Quantitative Analysis*, Vol. 48/6, pp. 1663-1692, https://doi.org/10.1017/s0022109014000015. [19]

Gilson, R. (2014), *The Nordic Model of Corporate Governance: The Role of Ownership*, SNS Publishing, https://scholarship.law.columbia.edu/faculty_scholarship/1895/. [16]

Implementeringsrådet (2026), *Implementeringsrådets rekommendationer om genomförande av ny EU-förordning om granskning av utländska direktinvesteringar*, https://implementeringsradet.se/wp-content/uploads/2026/02/260216FDITillganglighetsanpassat.pdf. [13]

Inspectorate of Strategic Products (2026), *FDI Screening Statistics*, https://isp.se/media/3y3is30a/statistik-2025-kv4-en-v3.pdf. [14]

Lekvall, P. (2014), *(ed.) The Nordic Corporate Governance Model*, SNS Publishing, https://snsse.cdn.triggerfish.cloud/uploads/2020/02/the_nordic_corporate_governance_model_1.pdf. [15]

Lidman, E. and R. Skog (2021), "London Allowing dual class Premium listings: A Swedish comment", *Journal of Corporate Law Studies*, Vol. 22/1, pp. 83-114, https://doi.org/10.1080/14735970.2021.1968993. [21]

Nenova, T. (2003), *The Value of Corporate Voting Rights and Control: A Crosscountry Analysis*, The Journal of Financial Economic 68 (2003), https://www.sciencedirect.com/science/article/pii/S0304405X03000692. [17]

OECD (2025), *Investment policy developments in 62 economies between 16 February 2024 and 15 March 2025*, OECD Publishing, Paris, https://doi.org/10.1787/1fd98ccf-en. [11]

OECD (2025), *The Swedish Equity Market: Institutional Framework and Trends*, OECD Publishing, Paris, https://doi.org/10.1787/0640a75c-en. [1]

OECD (2024), *The Swedish Corporate Bond Market: Challenges and Policy Recommendations*, OECD Publishing, Paris, https://doi.org/10.1787/7ff1a6ce-en. [7]

OECD (2022), *The Swedish Corporate Bond Market and Bondholder Rights*, OECD Capital Market Series, OECD Publishing, Paris, https://doi.org/10.1787/c443352d-en. [6]

Pagano, M., F. Panetta and L. Zingales (1998), "Why Do Companies Go Public? An Empirical Analysis", *The Journal of Finance*, Vol. 53/1, pp. 27-64, https://doi.org/10.1111/0022-1082.25448. [18]

Robeco (2024), *Country Sustainability Ranking*, https://www.robeco.com/en-int/sustainable-investing/expertise/most-sustainable-countries-in-the-world. [5]

SolAbility (2025), *The Global Sustainable Competitiveness Index 2025*, SolAbility Sustainable Intelligence, https://solability.com/pdfs/The%20Global%20Sustainable%20Competitiveness%20Index%20Report%202025.pdf. [4]

Soumitra Dutta, B. (ed.) (2023), *Global Innovation Index 2023: Innovation in the face of uncertainty*, https://www.wipo.int/edocs/pubdocs/en/wipo-pub-2000-2023-en-main-report-global-innovation-index-2023-16th-edition.pdf. [3]

The Swedish Act on Trading in Financial Instruments (1991), *Lag (1991:980) om handel med finansiella instrument*, https://www.riksdagen.se/sv/dokument-och-lagar/dokument/svensk-forfattningssamling/lag-1991980-om-handel-med-finansiella_sfs-1991-980/. [8]

The Swedish Companies Act (2005), *Aktiebolagslagen (2005:551)*, https://www.riksdagen.se/sv/dokument-och-lagar/dokument/svensk-forfattningssamling/aktiebolagslag-2005551_sfs-2005-551/. [10]

The Swedish Foreign Direct Investment Act (2023), *Lag (2023:560) om granskning av utländska direktinvesteringar*, https://www.riksdagen.se/sv/dokument-och-lagar/dokument/svensk-forfattningssamling/lag-2023560-om-granskning-av-utlandska_sfs-2023-560/. [12]

The Swedish Takeover Act (2006), *Lag (2006:451) om offentliga uppköpserbjudanden på aktiemarknaden*, https://www.riksdagen.se/sv/dokument-och-lagar/dokument/svensk-forfattningssamling/lag-2006451-om-offentliga-uppkopserbjudanden-pa_sfs-2006-451/. [9]

Notes

[1] Based on M&A data provided by LSEG. Country classification according to the nation of the target company's primary stock exchange listing. Refers to completed or withdrawn offers. Excludes stake purchases, repurchases and self-tender or recapitalisation deals.

[2] Estimates obtained through soliciting partners in the public M&A practice of the following firms: Cederquist, Gernandt & Danielsson, Mannheimer Swartling, Roschier, and Vinge.

[3] Based on analysis of security-level holding data of investment funds reporting to the Financial Services Authority, available here: https://www.fi.se/sv/vara-register/fondinnehav-per-kvartal/.

2 Mapping the Swedish equity markets

This chapter provides a comprehensive mapping of the Swedish equity markets, both public and private. It presents data on the characteristics of listed companies, the market ownership structure and the main trends in the use of equity financing. It also offers a broader overview of the Swedish corporate sector and describes the investor ecosystem.

2.1. The public equity markets

At the end of 2025, there were 909 listed companies on the Swedish equity market, with a total market capitalisation of nearly USD 1.3 trillion. After the United Kingdom, this is the market with the largest number of listed companies among European peer countries. Total market capitalisation represents 194% of GDP, which is significantly higher than major economies such as France (115%), the United Kingdom (101%), the Netherlands (97%) and Germany (61%) (Figure 2.1).

Figure 2.1. Market capitalisation and number of listed companies, end-2025

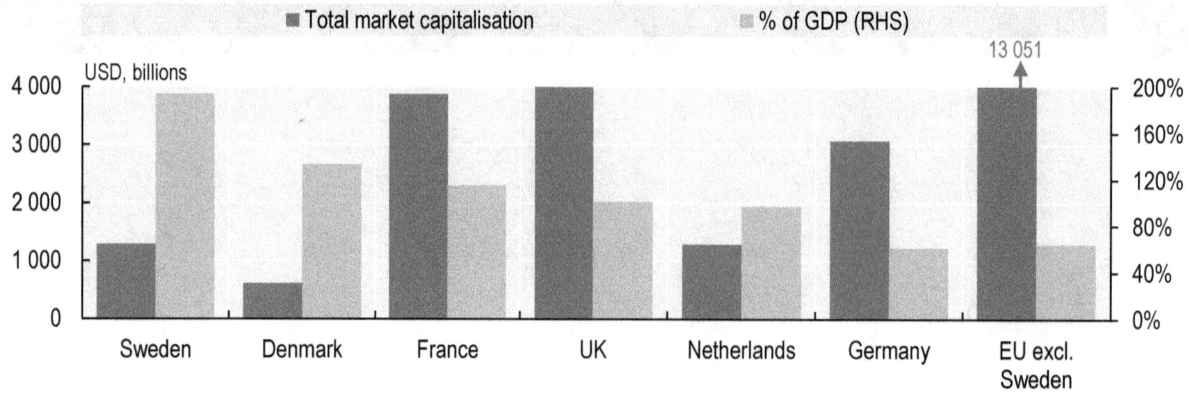

	Sweden	Denmark	France	UK	Netherlands	Germany	EU excl. Sweden
Number listed companies	909	146	640	1 379	96	744	4 420
...of which on MTFs	551	35	345	783	-	94	1477

Note: The number of companies listed on MTFs in the EU excluding Sweden is an estimate and should be considered a lower bound. For exchanges where LSEG data do not distinguish between market segments, all listed companies have been classified under the regulated market segment. MTF-listed companies include those listed on dedicated SME and growth-stage segments.
Source: OECD Capital Market Series dataset, LSEG and Bloomberg, see Annex for details; IMF.

The market comprises three main trading venues: Nasdaq Stockholm, Nordic Growth Market and Spotlight Stock Market. Nasdaq Stockholm, which is part of the Nasdaq group, serves as Sweden's primary exchange and is the largest in the Nordic region. It dominates the Swedish equity market with 685 listed companies representing over 99% of the country's total market capitalisation. Nasdaq Stockholm has a three-tier structure. The first tier is the main regulated market, which hosts 346 listed companies with a total market capitalisation of USD 1 254 billion. The First North Growth Market ("First North" hereafter), a multilateral trading facility (MTF), has two sub-segments: the premier market and the general market. Being an MTF, First North applies a different, less rigorous, set of rules for companies compared to the main market. However, the premier segment of First North is designed to increase the visibility of companies to investors and to help them prepare for a main market listing and therefore applies more stringent listing requirements. Between the launch of Nasdaq First North and 2023, more than 130 companies successfully moved to the main markets, with many using the premier segment as a stepping stone (Nasdaq, 2023[1]).

The two other markets, Nordic Growth Market (NGM) and Spotlight Stock Market, primarily focus on smaller, growth-oriented companies. NGM, a subsidiary of German Börse Stuttgart, operates a regulated market called Main Regulated, which currently lists twelve companies, and an MTF, NGM Nordic SME, with 88 listed companies. NGM's total market capitalisation amounts to USD 2.5 billion. Spotlight Stock Market operates as an MTF and has 124 listed companies with a total market capitalisation of USD 2.3 billion.

Figure 2.2. The Swedish public equity markets, end-2025

Trading venue	Segment type	Segment name	Number of companies	Market capitalisation (USD billion)
NASDAQ Stockholm	Regulated	Main Market	346	1 254
	MTF	First North Growth Market Premier	59	8.4
		First North Growth Market	280	14.9
Nordic Growth Market	Regulated	Main Market	12	1.0
	MTF	Nordic SME	88	1.5
Spotlight Stock Market	MTF		124	2.3
Total			**909**	**1282**

Source: OECD Capital Market Series dataset, LSEG and Bloomberg, see Annex for details.

The regulated Swedish equity markets are dominated by companies in the industrial and financial sectors, together representing over half of total market capitalisation. The composition is, however, very different on the MTFs, where technology and healthcare companies together account for more than half of both total market capitalisation and number of listed companies, suggesting these markets help provide financing to higher-risk, innovative ventures (Figure 2.3).

Figure 2.3. Industry composition of Swedish listed companies, end-2025

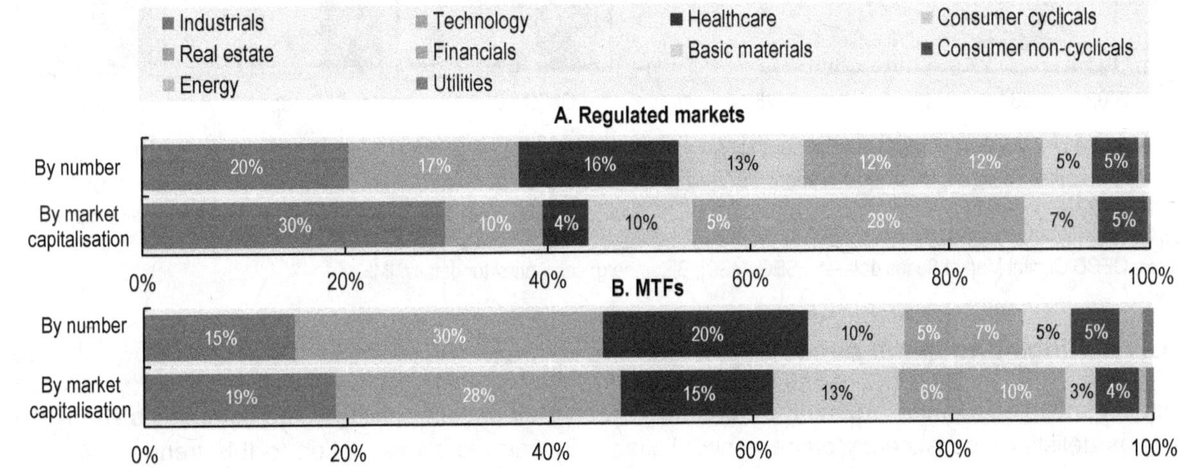

Source: OECD Capital Market Series dataset, LSEG and Bloomberg, see Annex for details.

2.1.1. Market performance

From an investor perspective, the Swedish market has been one of the best performing equity markets in the world historically. Since the early 2000s, the SIX Return Index (SIXRX), which tracks the performance of all listed companies on Nasdaq Stockholm, has consistently outperformed the total returns (accounting for both price changes and dividends) of major indices such as the S&P 500 in the United States and the STOXX 600 in Europe. Since 2002, this holds both in domestic currency (SEK) and USD terms (Figure 2.4, Panel A). This has naturally been an important factor in enhancing investor confidence and general interest in the market, attracting further investment and potentially reinforcing returns, creating a virtuous cycle.

The strong performance of the Swedish market is also reflected in its representation in international indices, notably in a European context. As shown in Panel B below, Swedish companies' weight in the MSCI Europe index (nearly 6%) is almost twice what its share in the constituent countries' aggregate GDP would suggest (less than 3%). It is also slightly overrepresented in OMXN40, which includes the 40 most traded companies in the Nordic region. In the MSCI World index, however, Sweden is in fact underweighted relative to its GDP share (Panel B). This is largely due to the heavy overrepresentation of the United States, which represents over 70% of the index. Only one other country is overrepresented relative to GDP (Switzerland).

Widespread inclusion in international indices is key to attracting a broad pool of investors, increasing the visibility of companies and markets. This is particularly important when it comes to institutional investors, which categorically have significantly larger ownership stakes in index-included companies compared to non-index companies across the world (Medina, de la Cruz and Tang, 2022[2]). The continued growth of passive, index-tracking investment strategies has intensified these dynamics.

Figure 2.4. Swedish market performance and representation in international indices

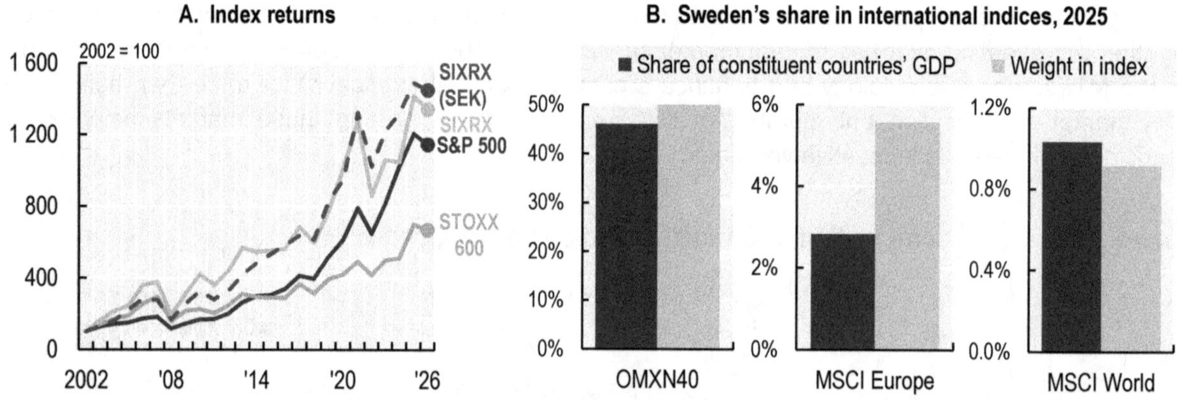

Note: In Panel A, index returns are in USD terms, unless otherwise stated, and include dividends. Data as of March 2026. In Panel B, GDP shares are calculated using information as of end 2025. Weighs in the indices are as of November 2025 for MSCI Europe and MSCI World and as of March 2026 for OMXN40. Country classification is based on country of listing. The number of firms in each index are (in order of appearance from left to right): 40, 404, 1 321.
Source: OECD Capital Market Series dataset, LSEG, MSCI, Bloomberg; see Annex for details; IMF.

2.1.2. Listings and initial public offerings

Most advanced economies around the world have seen their pool of publicly listed companies shrink over time, as delistings consistently outpace new listings. Sweden is an exception to this trend, having had positive net listings (new listings minus delistings) in the past decade. Since 2014, 1 114 companies have listed on the Swedish market, compared to 615 delistings, resulting in a net increase of 499 companies (Figure 2.5, Panels A and B). In 2021, a record year, more than 180 companies joined both regulated markets and MTFs. By comparison, the EU excluding Sweden has seen net delistings in almost every year between 2014 and 2025, for a total net loss of 986 companies (Panel C). The positive listing trend in Sweden is widespread and applies to almost all market segments, although most activity has taken place on Nasdaq Stockholm. From 2014-2025, 243 companies listed on Nasdaq's regulated segment, compared to 132 delistings. First North had more than 515 new listings, compared to 236 delistings. However, net listings on First North turned negative in 2023 and have remained negative since, for a net loss of 51 companies, and 66 on all MTFs.

Figure 2.5. Net listings by market

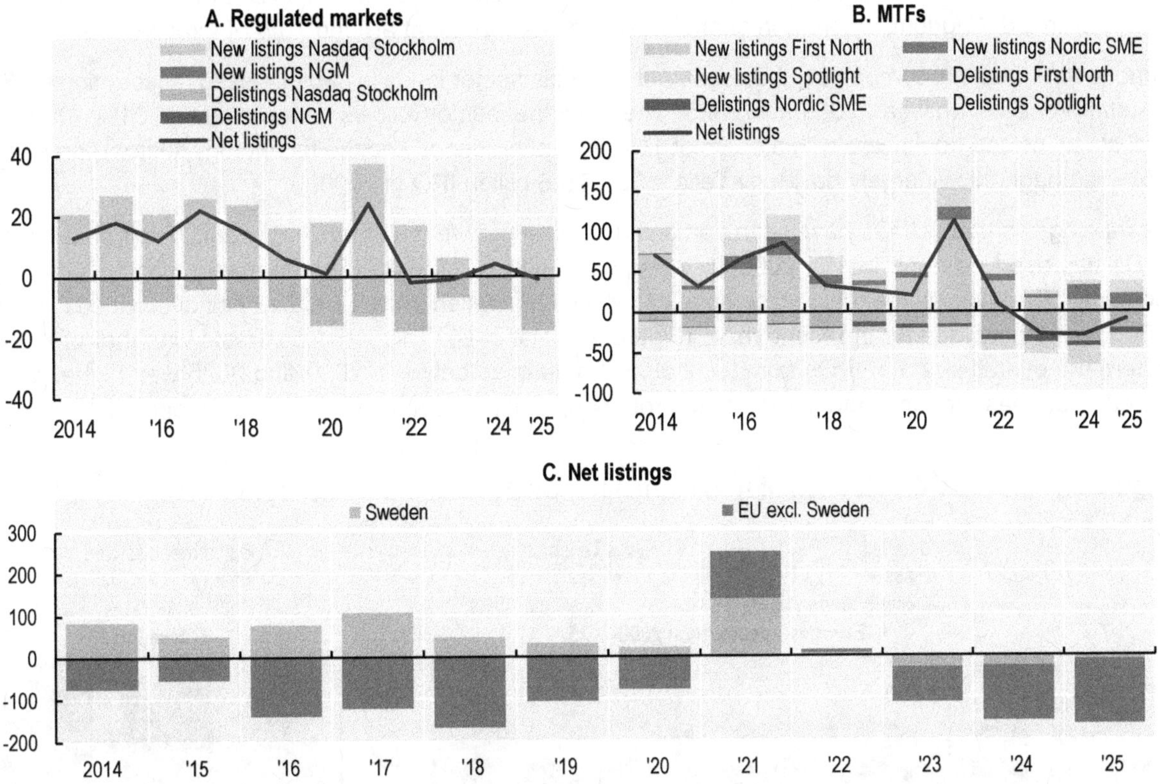

Note: NGM = Nordic Growth Market. Panel C refers to all markets (regulated and MTFs). EU-wide data are collected from ORBIS (before 2020) and LSEG (thereafter); country classifications for these data refer to corporate headquarters. See endnotes for commentary on data used in this figure.

Source: Nasdaq Stockholm/First North; Nordic Growth Market; Spotlight; OECD Capital Market Series dataset, LSEG, ORBIS.

A notable feature of the Swedish markets is the widespread use of public equity financing by smaller companies. Between 2000 and 2025, the median initial public offering (IPO) size was just USD 9 million, the smallest among peer countries, around a third of the size in the United Kingdom and France, and well below the EU median of USD 20 million. This primarily reflects strong activity on Swedish growth markets (Figure 2.6, Panel B).

Figure 2.6. IPOs by non-financial companies

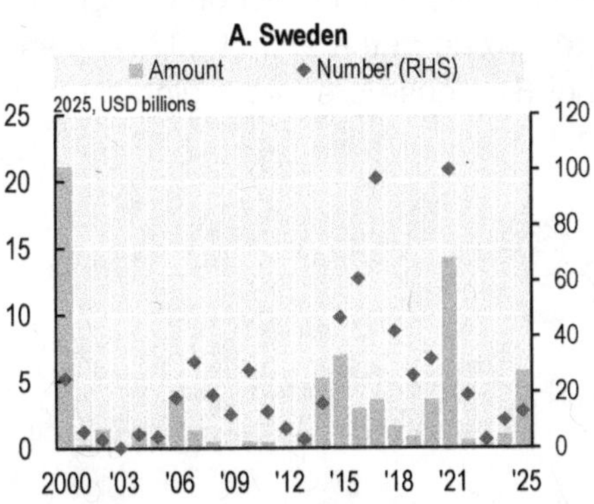

B. European peers, total 2000-2025

	Capital raised, % of GDP	Capital raised (USD millions)	Number of IPOs	Median IPO size (USD millions)	Non-financial IPOs, % over total
Sweden	0.48%	78 583	640	9	89%
UK	0.33%	341 864	2 123	23	70%
Denmark	0.18%	21 240	106	15	74%
Germany	0.15%	182 774	657	58	90%
Netherlands	0.15%	43 613	45	559	67%
France	0.14%	121 588	592	25	89%
EU	0.16%	746 329	3 911	20	84%

Note: In Panel B, amounts (capital raised and median size) are expressed in 2025 USD millions. The rightmost column shows the share of non-financial IPOs in total IPO proceeds.

Source: OECD Capital Market Series dataset, LSEG, Bloomberg, FactSet, see Annex for details; IMF.

Non-financial companies have been the main drivers of Swedish IPO activity, representing 89% of total proceeds raised in the 2000-25 period. This share is significantly higher than in Denmark, the Netherlands and the United Kingdom, where non-financial companies represent around 70% of total proceeds.

Among non-financial companies, the consumer cyclicals sector leads in capital raised, accounting for 32% of total proceeds between 2000 and 2025. The industrial sector follows with a share of 21%. Other key industries include healthcare with a share of 14% of total proceeds and the technology sector representing 15%, although this is largely driven by Telia's SEK 76.6 billion IPO in 2000.

Technology company IPOs have seen particularly strong growth over time in Sweden. Their share in total IPOs has risen from just 5% in 2008-15 to almost a fifth in 2016-25. The corresponding reduction has primarily been in consumer cyclical companies, which have fallen from more than half of proceeds in 2008-15 to less than a quarter in recent years (Figure 2.7, Panel B). This trend contrasts with that of the EU, where the overall share of IPOs from technology companies between 2000 and 2025 was higher than in Sweden but has remained largely stable at around 16% during both periods (2008-15 and 2016-25).

Figure 2.7. Industry distribution of non-financial IPOs by total proceeds, 2000-2025

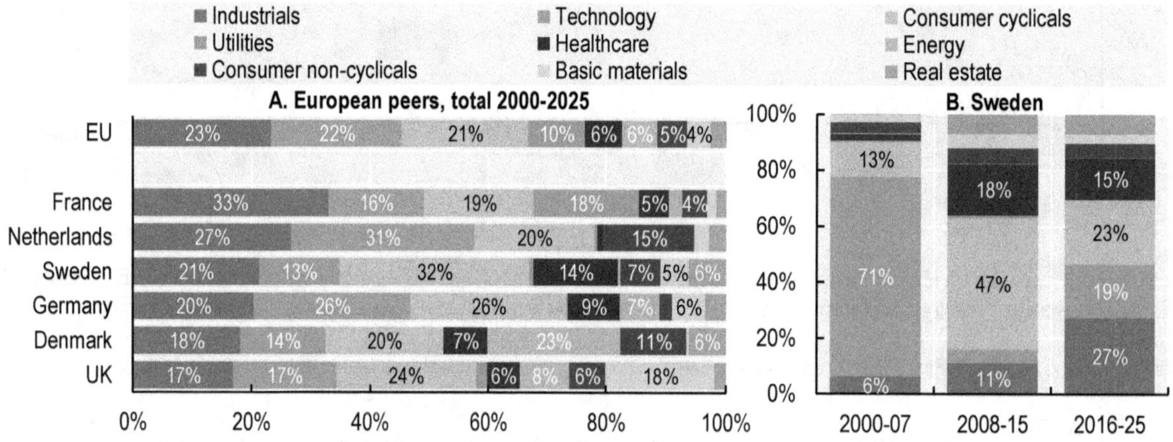

Source: OECD Capital Market Series dataset, LSEG, Bloomberg, FactSet, see Annex for details.

The Swedish markets have attracted a number of foreign listings in recent years. At the end of 2025, a total of 28 non-Swedish companies were listed on Nasdaq Stockholm and Spotlight, with an average market capitalisation of USD 792 million (Figure 2.8, Panel A). Most of these were Danish (12), Maltese (6), British (3) and Swiss (2). Notably, more than three-quarters of these companies are listed on the Swedish MTF markets. Conversely, it is relatively rare for Swedish companies to list on foreign stock exchanges. A total of ten Swedish-domiciled companies were listed abroad at the end of 2025, of which six in the United States, four of which on a US main market (Panel B). These are large, globally active companies with an average market capitalisation of USD 1.1 billion.

Figure 2.8. Number of cross-border listings, end 2025

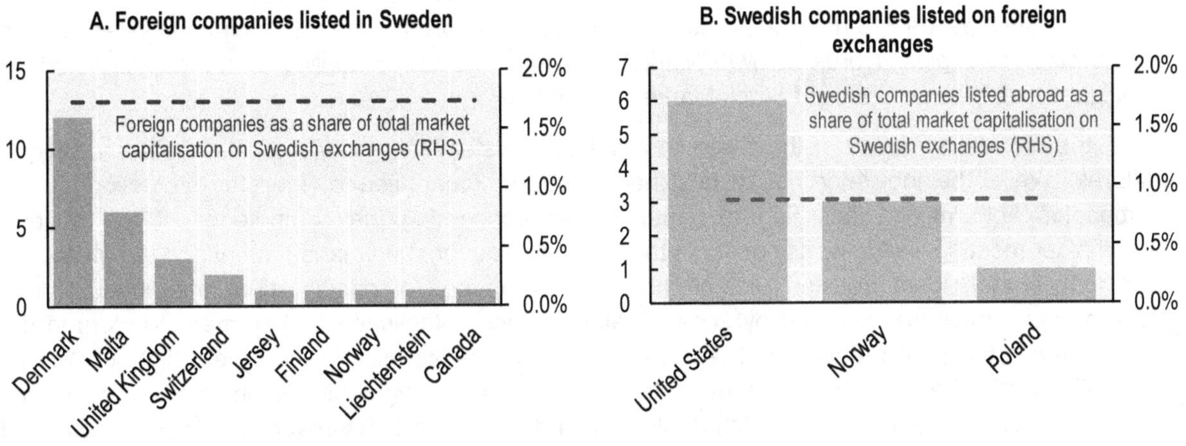

Source: OECD Capital Market Series dataset, LSEG, Bloomberg, Factset, see Annex for details.

Box 2.1. Regulation of listed companies and IPOs

As in all EU member states, listed companies and IPOs in Sweden are predominantly regulated by EU law, including the Listing Directive, the Transparency Directive, MiFID II, the Prospectus Regulation and the Market Abuse Regulation. However, there are important design aspects of the applicable domestic regulation of listed companies and IPOs in Sweden that may have contributed to the high levels of activity on local equity markets.

First, in areas where EU regulation leaves flexibility for member states regarding implementation and supervision, Sweden has generally not chosen to implement less stringent rules for listings and listed companies, focusing instead on strengthening investor protection. For example, Sweden has one of the lowest nationally decided thresholds for when a prospectus is required in a security offering, of EUR 2.5 million, compared to a range between EUR 5 to 8 million, the maximum allowed in the Prospectus Regulation, common in most other member states (ESMA, 2023[3]). Furthermore, in many areas national law offers significantly stronger investor protection than what is required both by EU law and in other markets. This notably includes strong shareholder rights. Shareholders in Sweden will almost always have the right to decide, through the general shareholder meeting, on company matters and overrule the board of directors. Pre-emptive rights are strong, shareholders have the exclusive right to decide on director pay and ultimately a right to, at any time and for any reason, call for an extraordinary general shareholder meeting and replace the board of directors. Previous studies have suggested Sweden has among the lowest measurable agency costs in international comparisons (Nenova, 2003[4]).

Second, and of particular interest given the important role of MTFs in Sweden (see section 2.1.6), many areas of the Swedish regulatory framework apply equally to companies listed on regulated markets and MTFs. This includes many areas where EU law only applies to companies on a regulated market, but where the scope of application also extends to MTFs in Sweden, such as the regulation on takeovers (implementing the Takeover Directive), rules on related party transactions and share issuance, as well as say on pay (implementing the Shareholder Rights Directive). Reporting standards are also largely aligned between venues, although there are some differences in accounting framework requirements. For example, on First North, only companies listed on the Premier segment are required to report using International Financial Reporting Standards (IFRS), the standard applicable to all companies on the main market. The remaining companies on First North can use local accounting standards (Nasdaq[5]). Similarly, companies listed on the Nordic SME market are allowed to use accounting frameworks other than IFRS, such as the K-3 rules, a Swedish accounting standard mandated for companies exceeding certain size thresholds (Nordic Growth Market, 2024[6]). The same applies to companies listed on Spotlight Stock Market (Spotlight Stock Market, 2023[7]) .

Third, the broader structure of the Swedish regulatory system for equity markets has some unique features. While the legislator has established a strong foundation of investor protection in the Companies Act, mainly consisting of general rules concerning the competence of the general shareholder meeting, including its control of the board of directors and management and the protection of minority shareholders, detailed rules are not laid down in the Companies Act or other in legislation. Instead, these rules are provided by self-regulatory bodies established by key market actors in co-operation with the public legislator. These self-regulatory bodies include the Swedish Stock Market Regulation Committee, which has the mandate to issue any rules concerning listed companies deemed necessary to protect market integrity (currently including the Swedish Takeover Code, rules on directed share issuances and rules concerning director and management remuneration); the Swedish Corporate Governance Board, which issues and monitors adherence to the Swedish Corporate Governance Code; and the Swedish Securities Council, which interprets and grants exemptions to the rules issued by the Stock Market Regulation Committee and Swedish Corporate Governance Board. The Securities Council can also rule on any other matter pertaining to a Swedish listed company not covered by other rules, which gives the market access to a rapid and cost-efficient dispute resolution system that can adapt to new market developments and innovations. In addition, access to the Securities Council means that court trials concerning disputes relating to, for example, takeovers, mergers, governance disputes or shareholder rights actions very rarely occur.

It should be emphasised that while the regulation referred to as "self-regulation" is issued by non-governmental entities, there are legal mechanisms and competence delegations in place that give the bodies within the self-regulatory system statutory mandates. For example, the rules and the rulings by the Securities Council are binding for listed companies, and breaches can be sanctioned.

2.1.3. Secondary public offerings

Secondary public offerings (SPOs) allow already listed companies to raise additional equity when needed. The possibility of doing so is a key benefit of being a listed company, enabling companies to weather temporary downturns while meeting their obligations to employees, creditors and suppliers. SPOs have played a particularly important role during recent times of financial stress. In 2010, in the aftermath of the global financial crisis, when bank lending contracted, non-financial companies in Sweden raised a record USD 12 billion in new equity through public equity markets. The same dynamics occurred during the COVID-19 pandemic, with non-financial companies raising USD 12.9 billion through SPOs in 2020 and a further record USD 16.8 billion in 2021 (Figure 2.9, Panel A). The growth in SPOs is not, however, just an effect of post-crisis issuance. Globally, total amounts issued through SPOs have trended upwards in the last three decades.

The number of SPOs has also increased, from an average of 33, amounting to USD 4.9 billion per year in the period from 2000-08 to 200 SPOs and USD 7.6 billion since 2009 (Figure 2.9, Panel A). On aggregate, Swedish companies made 3 689 SPOs between 2000 and 2025, the second highest number among peer countries, surpassed only by the United Kingdom. This represents almost one-third of the 11 557 SPOs carried out in EU on aggregate. In terms of capital raised, however, it represents only 8% of total EU figures, owing to widespread use of SPOs by smaller companies in Sweden. Relative to its economy, Sweden has the highest SPO activity among peer countries, reaching 1% of GDP, more than twice the EU aggregate. This activity is primarily driven by non-financial companies, which account for 80% of total SPO proceeds since 2000, 15 percentage points more than in the EU aggregate (Panel B).

Figure 2.9. SPOs by non-financial companies

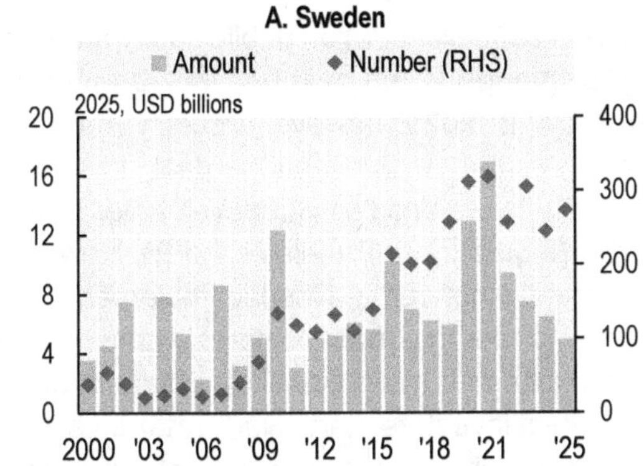

B. European peers, total 2000-2025

	Capital raised, % of GDP	Capital raised (USD millions)	Number of SPOs	Non-financial SPOs, % over total
Sweden	1.0%	173 375	3 689	80%
UK	0.9%	836 063	11 002	60%
Denmark	0.8%	89 192	386	75%
Netherlands	0.6%	166 509	341	68%
France	0.6%	520 468	2 000	77%
Germany	0.4%	459 458	1 596	72%
EU	0.4%	2136 254	11 557	65%

Note: In Panel B, capital raised is expressed in 2025 USD millions. The rightmost column shows the share of non-financial SPOs in total SPO proceeds.
Source: OECD Capital Market Series dataset, LSEG, Bloomberg, FactSet, see Annex for details; IMF.

Box 2.2. Swedish SPO regulation

An SPO can provide pre-emptive rights to existing shareholders, giving them the option to buy newly issued shares before other investors. In Sweden, the basic rules governing this process, along with SPO issuance more broadly, are laid out in the Swedish Companies Act. The law takes a rather stringent approach to directed share issues. These are only allowed when the divergence from the shareholders' pre-emptive rights is justified by the business' commercial interests and approved by the general shareholder meeting with a two-thirds majority of the share capital – not only votes (the use of dual class shares is widespread in Sweden, see section 2.4). This gives single-vote shareholders significant influence in companies with dual class share structures. Additionally, if the individuals entitled to subscribe to the shares include board members, executives or employees, along with their close relatives and entities they influence, a nine-tenths majority of both shares and votes is required. Complementing the legal requirements, the Swedish Stock Market Regulation Committee has issued additional and more detailed rules concerning directed share issuances, which in turn are interpreted by the Swedish Securities Council.

This regulatory model, where statutory principles are built upon and supplemented through delegated regulation, allows the Securities Council to review and approve (or reject) more complex structures, where there may be doubts about the compliance with fundamental company law principles, before they are executed. This allows for a great deal of flexibility in terms of transaction structures, which may help explain the very high frequence of smaller SPOs in Sweden.

2.1.4. Market liquidity

The level of secondary market liquidity is an important determinant of the efficiency and functioning of a public equity market. A liquid market also promotes efficient price formation and reduces price volatility. A lack of liquidity therefore leads to higher transaction costs, in turn raising companies' cost of capital. Low levels of liquidity can also serve to undermine investor confidence and may discourage market participation, by restricting investors' ability to exit their investment at a time of their choosing at a price that aligns with those publicly available. Liquid markets tend to create a virtuous cycle, with empirical studies indicating that increased liquidity in secondary markets encourages companies to list and issue additional equity, thereby contributing to the further development of the public equity market (Hanselaar, Stulz and van Dijk, 2019[8]).

Measured by the turnover ratio (total traded value over total market capitalisation) on public equity markets, liquidity has been on a declining trend on the main Swedish exchange in the past decade. On Nasdaq Stockholm, the ratio fell from over 60% in 2014 to 41% in 2024. In 2025, however, liquidity improved modestly, with the turnover ratio rising to 45%. Based on international stock exchange data, this ranks Sweden second among peer countries. The MTF segment First North has seen similar developments, with turnover falling from over 60% in 2020 to just over 30% in 2024 (Figure 2.10, Panels A and B). However, in 2025 it rebounded to 57%. In January 2024, in response to liquidity concerns, Nasdaq implemented an auction model for shares listed on the First North Growth Market. Under this model, shares with a bid-ask spread exceeding 7% on average for two consecutive quarters must either hire a liquidity provider or adopt a trading system with five daily auctions. This initiative aims to protect investors, particularly retail investors, from the high price volatility associated with less liquid stocks, which can weaken market confidence (Nasdaq, 2023[9]).

Figure 2.10. Secondary stock market liquidity, 2025

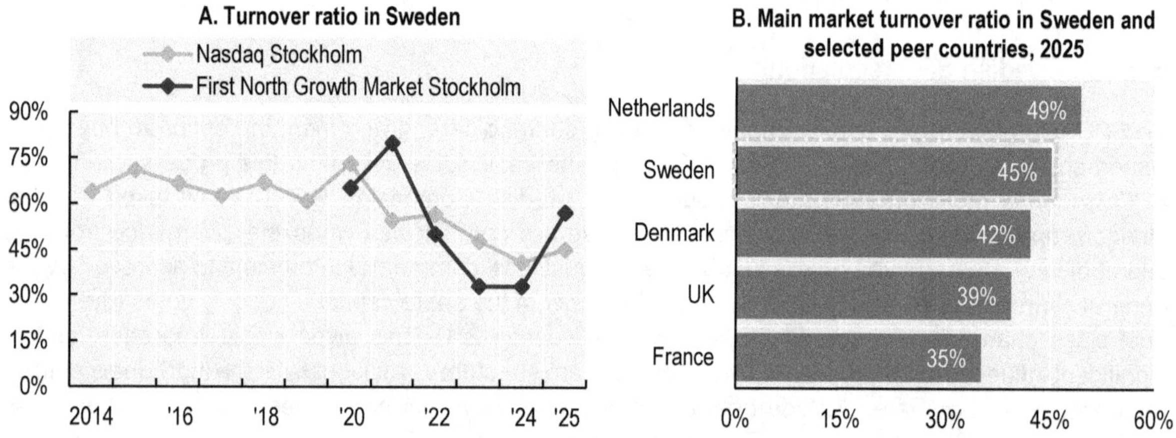

Note: Turnover is calculated as the ratio of traded value to total market capitalisation.
Source: Euronext; LSE; Nasdaq Stockholm; Nasdaq Copenhagen.

It is important to note, however, that a decline in the turnover ratio on public markets does not necessarily imply a reduction in overall trading activity. Recent years have seen an increase in fragmentation in trading, driven by technological advances and regulatory changes, with trades commonly spread across several venues rather than being concentrated on a single exchange. For example, a significant amount of trading now takes place in off-exchange dark pools (Hagströmer, 2022[10]; OECD, 2016[11]). In addition, electronic communication networks provide platforms for efficiently matching buy and sell orders outside traditional exchanges (Flicker, 2004[12]). The stock market turnover ratio only reflects trading that takes place on the stock exchange. A decline in this ratio can therefore reflect a re-orientation of activity away from traditional exchanges rather than decreases in total trading activity.

Secondary market liquidity is partly influenced by the free float ratio (the portion of a company's total shares available for trading). A lower free float is typically associated with a lower turnover ratio. The market capitalisation-weighted free float ratio in Sweden is 76%, which is in the middle of the distribution among peer countries (Figure 2.11). This is partly an effect of the prominence of family-owned investment companies in Sweden, which play a central role in the country's capital markets. These companies often retain significant ownership stakes, leaving a smaller proportion of shares available for public trading and thus contributing to a lower free float (even if family ownership often represents a much more significant share of votes than of market capitalisation, see sections 2.4 and 2.6). Only 33% of stocks in Sweden have a free float ratio above 75%, which is comparatively low (Figure 2.11, Panel B).

Figure 2.11. Free float levels in Sweden and peer countries, end-2025

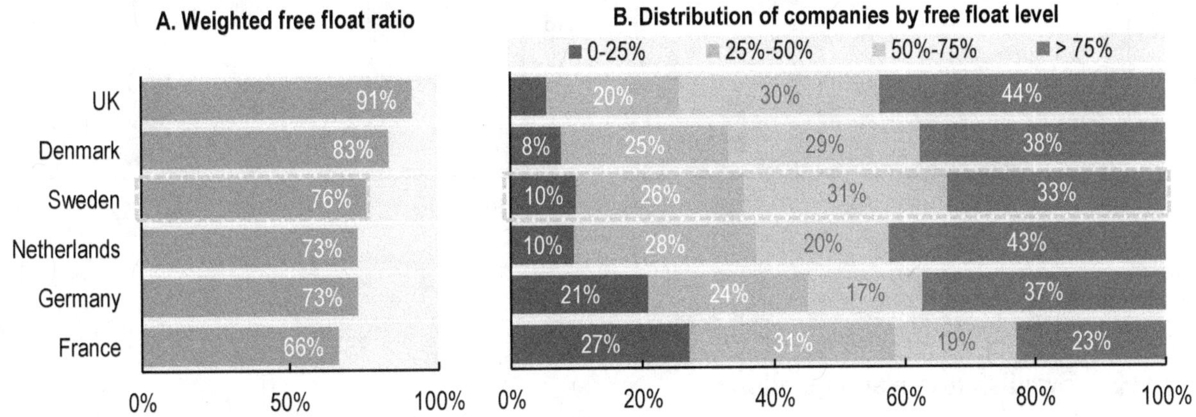

Note: In Panel A, the free float ratio is weighted by market capitalisation.
Source: OECD Capital Market Series dataset, LSEG and Bloomberg; see Annex for details.

2.1.5. Takeovers

There is significant takeover activity on the Swedish public equity markets, partly underpinned by the domestic regulatory structure (see Box 2.3). While the number of takeovers has fluctuated significantly, it has been on a general upward trend over time. Between 2010 and 2016, Swedish marketplaces saw an average of 15 takeovers per year, rising to 22 per year between 2017 and 2025. In value terms, the average deal volume rose from USD 7 billion to USD 11 billion over the same periods. Takeovers involving target companies listed on an MTF have become more common over time. However, as expected given the smaller size of the target companies, these transactions account for a larger share of the total number of deals than of their overall value (Figure 2.12).

In 2023, total deal volume dropped to USD 21 billion, the lowest level since 2013. However, 2024 saw a sharp rebound, reaching a record 28 deals and a total value of USD 14 billion. Macroeconomic factors such as falling interest rates have contributed to this recovery, with rising IPO activity, greater participation from private equity and an increase in large strategic deals adding to positive momentum (EY, 2025[13]). While the number of deals in 2025 remained close to the record level reached in 2024, total deal value fell by more than one third, reflecting a higher share of takeovers involving companies listed on MTFs.

Figure 2.12. Takeovers on Swedish equity markets

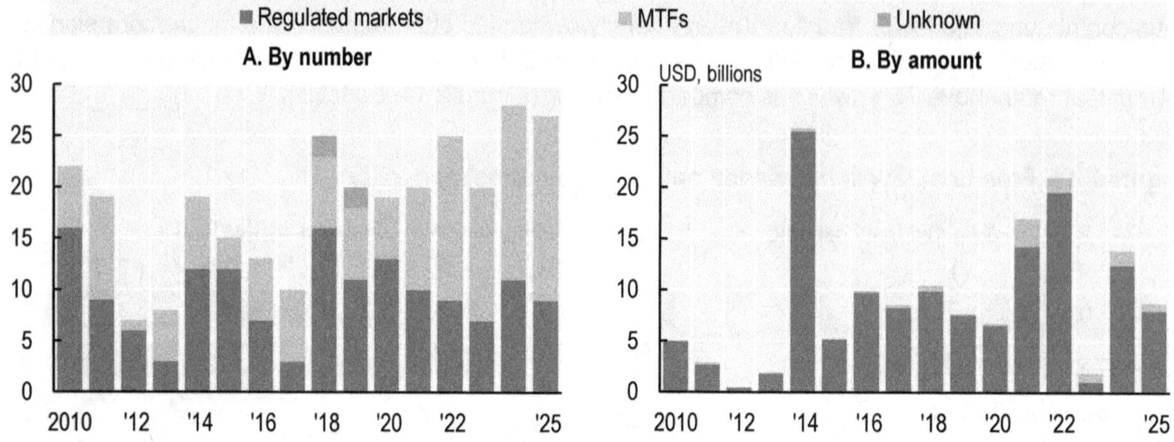

Source: Swedish Securities Council.

> **Box 2.3. Swedish takeover regulation**
>
> The Swedish takeover regulation follows the same delegated regulatory structure described in Box 2.1 and Box 2.2. Certain basic rules (primarily results of implementing the EU Takeover Directive) are laid down in the Swedish Takeover Act, while most detailed rules are found in the Takeover Rules issued by the Swedish Stock Market Regulation Committee. The Swedish Securities Council can interpret the Takeover Rules and grant dispensations in individual cases, with delegated authority from the Swedish Financial Services Authority.
>
> A statement from the Council can usually be obtained within days and will rarely take more than two weeks. Quick and predictable access to binding statements concerning the compliance of a proposed bid structure, granting legal certainty, is viewed by practitioners as one of the key factors behind the high takeover activity in Sweden.

2.1.6. The role of MTFs in the Swedish equity market ecosystem

One of the key features of the Swedish public equity markets is the dynamism of the MTF markets. Two-thirds of all Swedish public companies (551) are listed on an MTF, and since 2014 nearly 80% (868) of the total number of new listings in Sweden have been on MTFs. This level of activity is much more significant than in most comparable countries. This has given smaller, higher risk, growth-oriented companies widespread access to public equity financing. There is evidence suggesting that this has helped drive innovation in Sweden which, according to the European Innovation Scoreboard, was the most innovative EU member state in 2025, having previously ranked first in 2018 and 2019, ahead of Denmark which led the ranking from 2020 to 2024 (European Commission, 2025[14]). However, despite the high number of companies listed on MTFs, their total market capitalisation is still relatively modest at just above USD 27 billion, representing only 2.1% of the Swedish total. The regulated markets – particularly Nasdaq Stockholm – remain by far the most significant venues (Figure 2.2).

Market participants have noted that many, though by no means all, companies opting to list on MTFs in Sweden could in fact qualify for listing directly on the regulated market. One reason they choose to list on MTFs instead is the faster, and therefore more cost-effective, listing process. Moreover, since the regulatory frameworks for both venues are broadly similar, with comparable listing requirements (see

Box 2.1), the difference in terms of investor demand between MTFs and regulated markets is, in some cases, not big enough to justify the additional costs of a regulated market listing. Relatively higher retail engagement in the MTFs compared to regulated markets helps support this dynamic, but there is also institutional investor presence on these markets, including domestic pension funds (see section 2.5.1).

A key aspect of the Swedish MTF markets is that they function as a stepping stone to listing on the regulated market. Since 2013, an average of 45% of new listings on regulated markets annually have come from an MTF (Figure 2.13). This is a critical point – this natural movement between growth and main markets means domestic companies have continuous access to equity funding throughout their development and creates a pipeline of companies for the main market, increasing investor interest, which, in turn, increases the incentives for companies to list on an MTF in the first place. This dynamic is partly an effect of the above-mentioned compliance with regulated market requirements by many MTF-listed companies (which follows from similar treatment in Swedish regulation), as well as a natural consequence of the large number of companies on the Swedish MTF market. Another factor might be a restriction under Swedish law which limits the trading of own shares to regulated markets, meaning MTF-listed companies are not permitted to conduct share buybacks (Finansinspektionen, 2016[15]). Some companies may opt to move to a regulated market to gain access to this option.

Figure 2.13. Share of new listings on Swedish regulated markets coming from an MTF

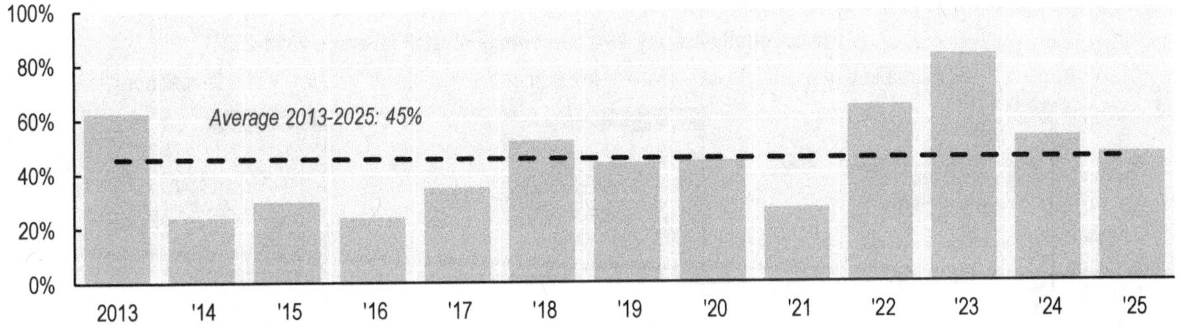

Source: Nasdaq Stockholm, Nordic Growth Market, First North Growth Market.

Another notable feature is the role of external advisors, mandated by the exchanges, that serve to help MTF companies in the listing process and to comply with market rules thereafter. This model is inspired by the Nominated Adviser (Nomad) system used on the London Stock Exchange's AIM market. Major MTF operators, notably Nasdaq First North ("certified advisers") and NGM Nordic SME ("mentors") impose a mandatory requirement to retain such advisers, at least for a certain period of time (Nasdaq, 2015[16]; Nordic Growth Market, 2024[6]). The advisers are certified by the exchange and can be, for example, corporate finance firms, accounting firms or investment banks. In the Nasdaq model, certified advisers operate under the exchange's rules to support companies listed on First North (including First North Premier). Certified advisers serve as intermediaries between the company and the exchange and are responsible for guiding companies through the listing process, ensuring they meet initial requirements, and assisting with ongoing compliance and disclosure obligations. Even after listing, certified advisers continue to monitor companies and provide support. This regulatory guidance helps companies navigate increasing regulatory complexity as they grow. In addition, certified advisers may offer trainings for corporate management and boards as well as updates on recent regulatory developments.

At the beginning of February 2026, 46 certified advisers were registered with Nasdaq, operating across the Nordic markets (Nasdaq, 2026[17]). A similar system applies on the NGM Nordic SME market, with sponsorship required for the first two years post-listing. The market had 25 registered mentor firms as of April 2025 (Nordnet[18]). The external adviser structure has helped simplify the listing process and strengthen corporate governance standards as well as improve operations among smaller listed companies.

2.2. The private equity market

Sweden has a globally significant private equity (PE) industry that is active both domestically and internationally. It is home to one of the world's largest PE firms by assets under management. The sector's economic impact is substantial. According to industry association statistics, PE firms own around 1 200 Swedish companies, employing 260 000 people (Riksbanken, 2024[19]). There is also considerable venture capital activity. Together with the active public markets, this provides Swedish companies with access to a diversity of domestic equity funding throughout the corporate lifecycle that is relatively rare among countries in the European Union.

Across a range of measures, Sweden represents a share of European PE activity that far exceeds its economic heft. In the past decade, Swedish PE firms have represented an average of 9% of European fundraising, 3.2 times more than its GDP share. In 2022, when Swedish funds represented over 16% of total fundraising, three of the top five largest funds closed in Europe were headquartered in Stockholm, the other two being in London (PitchBook, 2023[20]). Similarly, Swedish companies have received 60% more PE investment and been divested 95% more than GDP weight would suggest.[1] This outperformance has been consistent over time (Figure 2.14, Panels A and B).

Figure 2.14. Private equity activity in Sweden and peer countries

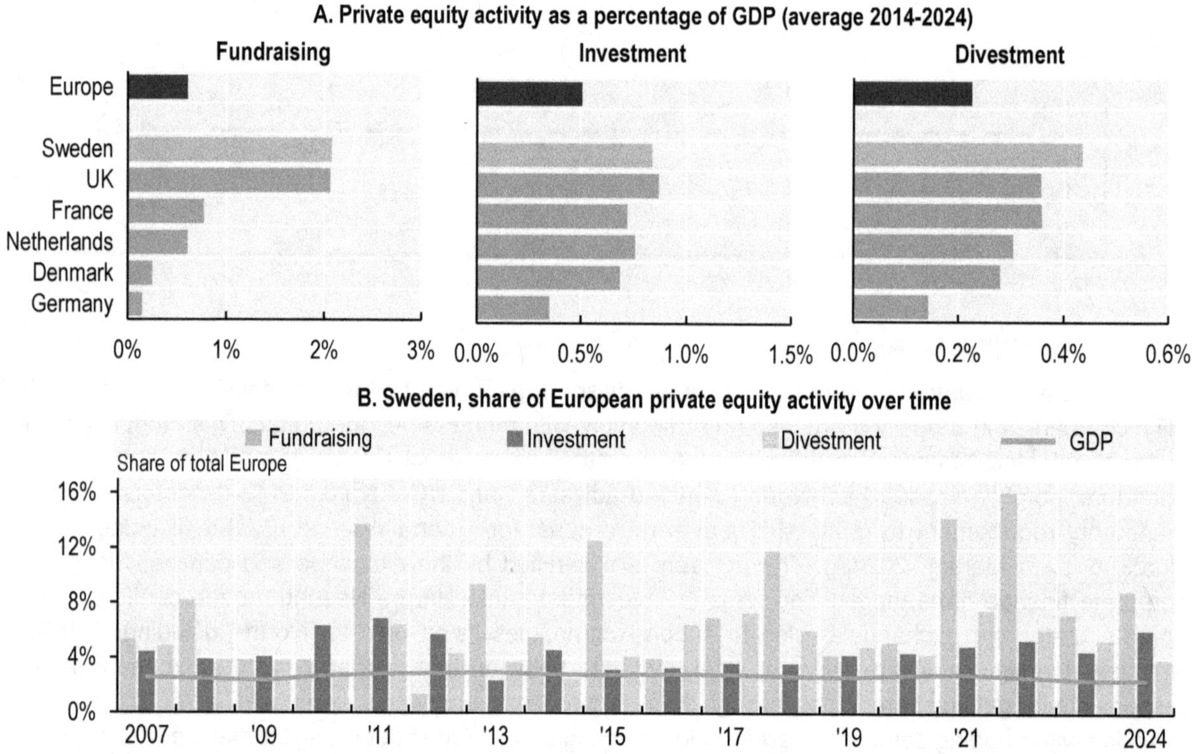

Note: "Europe" refers to all 27 EU member states, plus Bosnia and Herzegovina, Iceland, Liechtenstein, Montenegro, North Macedonia, Norway, San Marino, Serbia, Switzerland, Ukraine, the United Kingdom and the Vatican City. Fundraising by location of private equity firm advisory teams. Investment and divestment by location of portfolio firms.
Source: Invest Europe.

Given the size of the Swedish PE industry relative to its economy, the Swedish fundraising landscape is very international, with a substantial share of total fundraising coming from foreign investors. In the last six years, domestic investors have accounted for no more than 8% of aggregate fundraising, by far the lowest share among peer countries. Together with the United Kingdom, Swedish PE firms have the largest share of non-European investors (Figure 2.15). This reflects above all the global character of very large Swedish PE firms such as EQT and Nordic Capital.

Figure 2.15. Private equity fundraising by investor origin, total 2019-2024

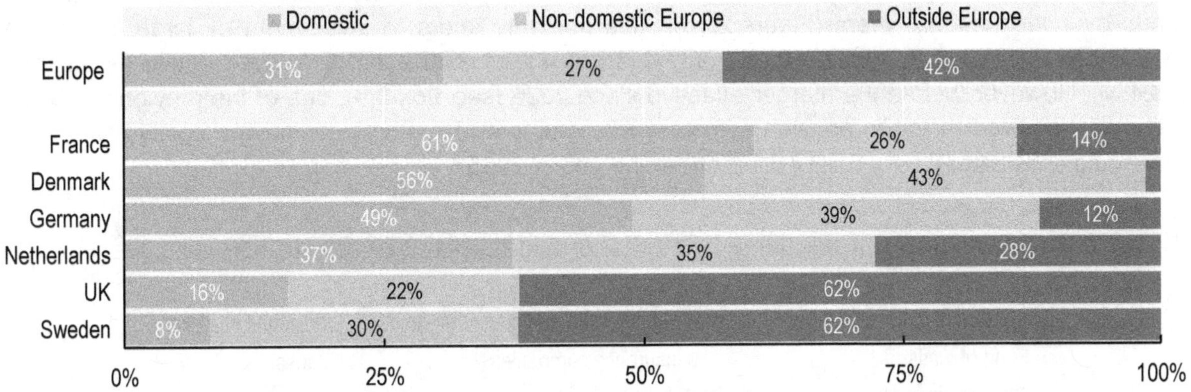

Note: The analysis only includes funds raised where the origin of the investor is specified. "Europe" refers to all 27 EU member states, plus Bosnia and Herzegovina, Iceland, Liechtenstein, Montenegro, North Macedonia, Norway, San Marino, Serbia, Switzerland, Ukraine, the United Kingdom and the Vatican City. By location of private equity firm advisory teams.
Source: Invest Europe.

Among the five PE firms that have raised the largest amount of money globally during the past five years, four are based in the United States and one in the EU. Stockholm-based EQT ranks second, having raised USD 113 billion (Table 2.1). The growth of EQT as a major global PE player reflects Sweden's long history of active family ownership (see also section 2.6). Its founding in 1994 followed from a mandate by Investor AB, the Wallenberg family's investment company and one of the oldest industrial holding companies in Europe. The fact that it was closely involved in the founding of EQT allowed the latter to draw from the industrial expertise of a long-term owner, facilitating the development of an investment model focused heavily on improving corporate operational performance that would grow to serve as the primary model for the global private equity industry.

Table 2.1. Top 5 private equity firms worldwide by fundraising amount, total 2020-2024

Firm	Headquarters	Amount raised (USD billions)
KRR	New York	118
EQT	Stockholm	113
Blackstone	New York	96
Thoma Bravo	Chicago	88
TPG	San Francisco	73

Note: Refers to the amount of private equity capital raised between 1 January 2020 and 31 December 2024.
Source: Private Equity International (2025[21]), PEI 300: The world's largest private equity firms, https://www.privateequityinternational.com/pei-300/#pei-300-full-ranking.

It is also notable that the banking industry has been part of this development from the beginning, both directly and indirectly. Not only is Investor AB a major owner of SEB, one of Sweden's largest banks, but SEB itself was one of the three initial backers of EQT, together with Investor AB and US PE firm AEA Investors (EQT[22]). The connection between the banking sector and the development of (non-bank) capital markets illustrate the dynamics through which the Swedish ownership model has fostered an environment where banks do not restrict the development of non-bank financing (even if Sweden remains a predominantly bank-based economy).

It is not just the nationality, but also the character, of the largest capital providers to Swedish PE firms that differs compared to many other countries in the EU. Uniquely among EU peer countries (but in line with the United Kingdom), pension funds have been the single largest investor category (32%) in Swedish PE funds over the past six years (Figure 2.16). This primarily refers to investment by large international pension funds. Swedish pension funds only allocate 4% of total asset to private equity (Riksbanken, 2024[19]). However, before the merger effective since 2026 (see Box 2.5), one of the previously six main funds in the Swedish public pension system, AP6, was focused entirely on private equity investments, managing SEK 84 billion (c. EUR 7.7 billion) at the end of 2025.

Figure 2.16. Private equity fundraising by capital provider, total 2019-2024

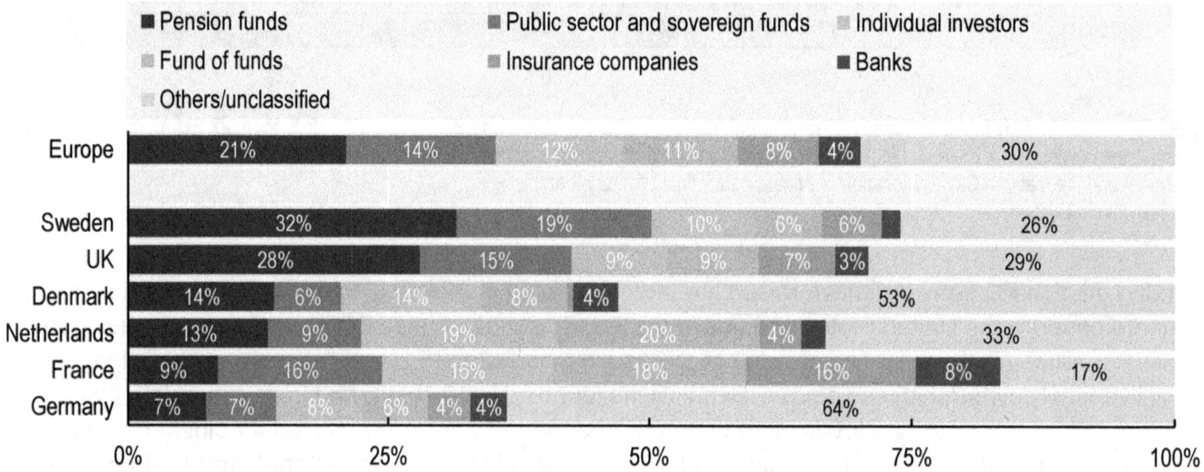

Note: "Europe" refers to all 27 EU member states, plus Bosnia and Herzegovina, Iceland, Liechtenstein, Montenegro, North Macedonia, Norway, San Marino, Serbia, Switzerland, Ukraine, the United Kingdom and the Vatican City. By location of private equity firm advisory teams.
Source: Invest Europe.

Like in other countries, buyout is by far the largest PE segment in Sweden, representing about three quarters of aggregate investment in the last decade, a share that has remained relatively stable over time. It is notable how much global PE investment in Swedish companies has picked up in the last five years. Total investment – buyout, growth, venture capital and other types – has more than doubled from an average of just above EUR 3 billion from 2007-18 to EUR 6.4 billion from 2019-2024 (Figure 2.17, Panels A and B). This is driven primarily by significant investments in 2021 and 2022, following a period of extensive monetary policy expansion and consequent low cost of debt. The reversal of such policies (most notably quantitative easing and near-zero policy rates) may lead to decreases in PE activity and lower exit multiples for investors.

Figure 2.17. Private equity investment in Sweden and selected peer countries

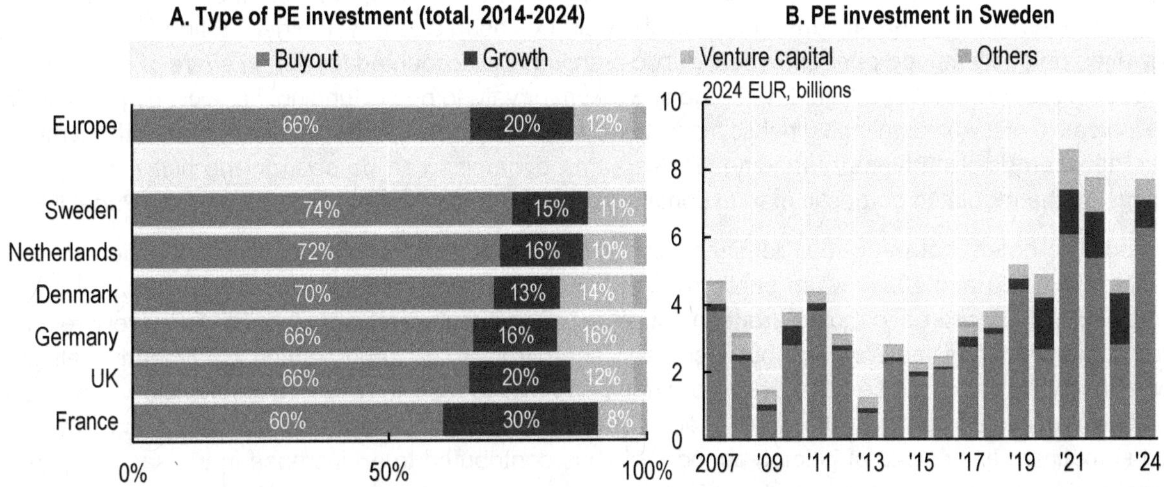

Note: "Europe" refers to all 27 EU member states, plus Bosnia and Herzegovina, Iceland, Liechtenstein, Montenegro, North Macedonia, Norway, San Marino, Serbia, Switzerland, Ukraine, the United Kingdom and the Vatican City. By location of portfolio firm.
Source: Invest Europe.

The industry distribution of Swedish firms receiving PE investment is largely in line with that in Europe more broadly (Figure 2.18). Biotech, healthcare, computer and electronics companies have received nearly half of total investment in the past six years – an indication of the role that external private equity, like its public market equivalent, can play in allocating funding to innovative ventures that have the possibility of enhancing economic productivity more broadly. Three industry groups – biotech, healthcare, computer and electronics; consumer goods and services; and business products and services– have received 78% of all PE investment in the last six years. Among these, the first is higher in Sweden than Europe on aggregate, whereas the second is significantly lower.

Figure 2.18. Private equity investment by industry, total 2019-2024

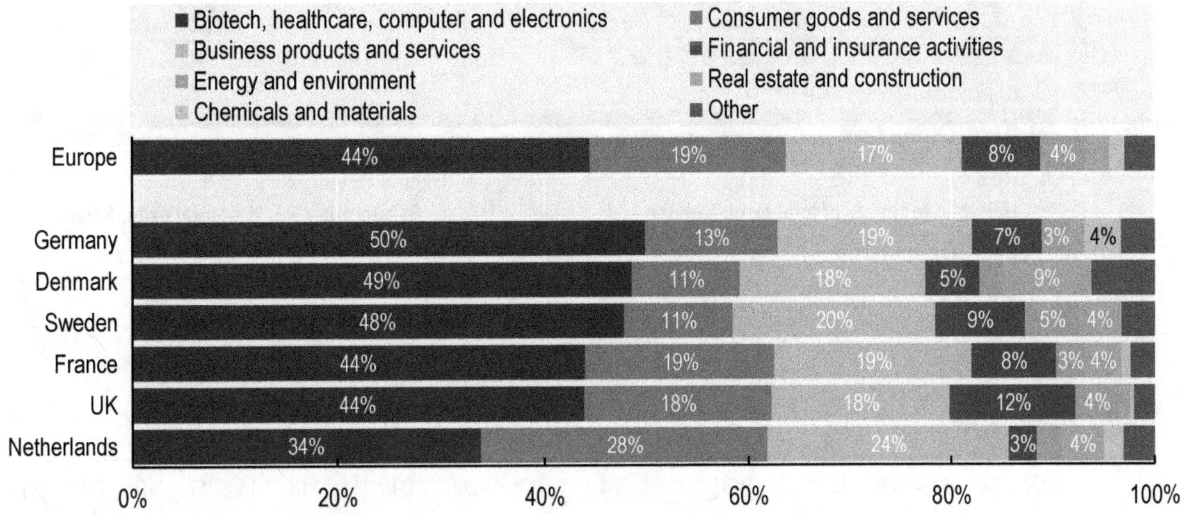

Note: "Europe" refers to all 27 EU member states, plus Bosnia and Herzegovina, Iceland, Liechtenstein, Montenegro, North Macedonia, Norway, San Marino, Serbia, Switzerland, Ukraine, the United Kingdom and the Vatican City. By location of portfolio firm.
Source: Invest Europe.

The way in which private equity firms exit their investments at the end of the holding period has important implications for capital markets more broadly. Similarly to all other European countries, the most common type of divestment of Swedish firms in the last six years has been a sale to another PE firm (30% by value). However, uniquely among peer countries, public listings have accounted for a high share of divestment in Sweden (25%) (Figure 2.19, Panel A). Large flows from private to public funding, i.e. exits by public listing, are indicative of a well-functioning public market and a dynamic broader market ecosystem without missing links between different types of funding. These same dynamics can be seen in the high share of new listings on the regulated domestic market coming from the growth market (see Figure 2.13, Panel B).

It should be noted, however, that dominant exit types change with market conditions. Public exits were common in 2020 and 2021, when public market valuations were favourable, but fell in 2022 (although remained high compared to most European countries). Conversely, sales to other PE firms were relatively less common during these years, but increased sharply in 2022, representing over nearly half of all divestments by value. Since 2011, the two exit types have tended to move inversely, with a correlation coefficient of -0.59 (Figure 2.10, Panels B and C). Recent years have seen an increase in intra-PE sales and sometimes extensions of holding period. This has contributed to an increase in transactions, known as secondaries, where existing investors (the limited partners) sell their stakes in the fund, often to manage liquidity needs (Bain & Company, 2024[23]). The same is true for so-called continuation funds, where sponsors sell their assets to a newly established fund instead of liquidating at the end of the initial term. Limited partners can then choose to transfer their investments into the new fund (Kastiel and Nili, 2024[24]).

Figure 2.19. Private equity divestment by exit forms

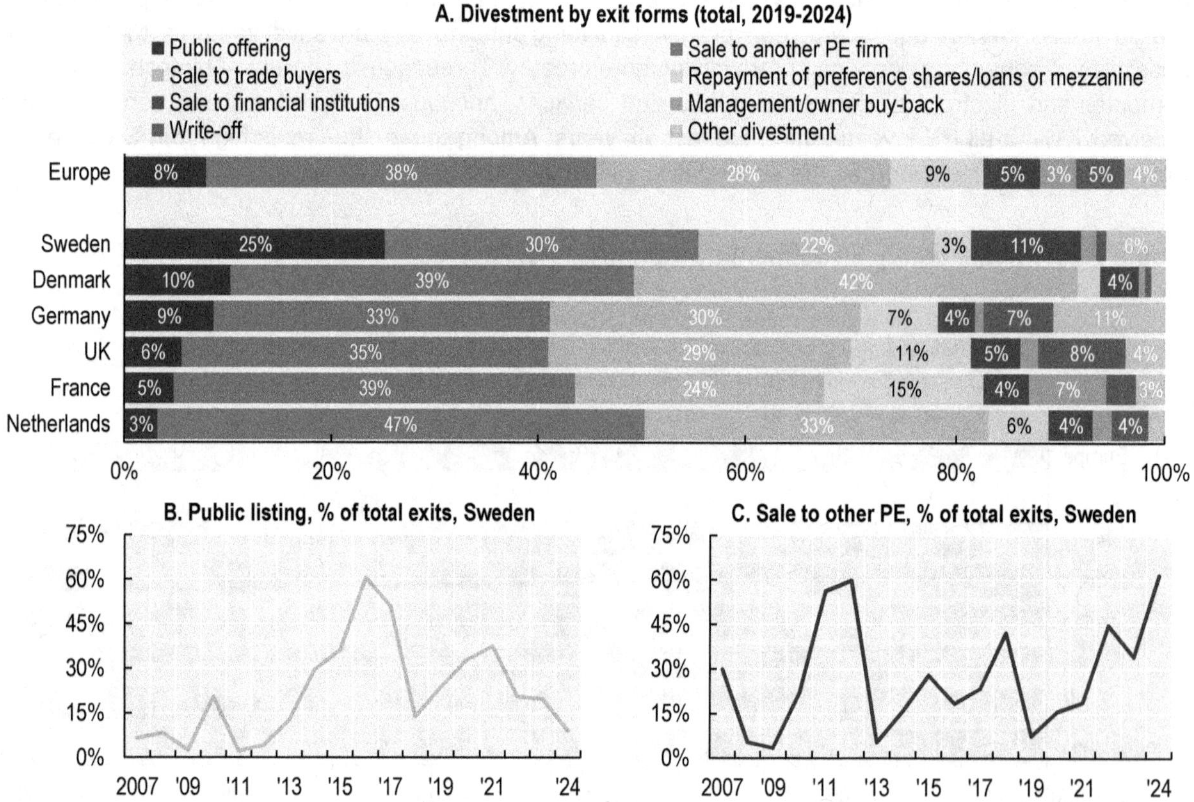

Note: "Europe" refers to all 27 EU member states, plus Bosnia and Herzegovina, Iceland, Liechtenstein, Montenegro, North Macedonia, Norway, San Marino, Serbia, Switzerland, Ukraine, the United Kingdom and the Vatican City. By location of portfolio firm. Shares are calculated based on deal value.
Source: Invest Europe.

While naturally a smaller part of the private equity market in absolute terms than buyout and growth, a vibrant venture capital (VC) industry is critical to the development of capital markets and to economic dynamism more broadly. Without risk-willing investment available for innovative ventures, an economy will eventually stagnate. In 2025, Stockholm-headquartered firms had the fourth highest total VC deal value among European cities at EUR 3.7 billion, behind London (EUR 23.8 billion), Paris (EUR 8.7 billion) and Berlin (EUR 4.7 billion) (PitchBook, 2026[25]; 2024[26]). The level of VC investment into Swedish firms is also relatively high in a European context. VC investment as a share of GDP has averaged 0.12% in the last six years, the third highest among peer countries after Denmark (0.13%) and the United Kingdom (0.14%). Like the larger, mature PE segment, VC saw sharp growth in 2021 and 2022. Seed investment – funding of companies at the earliest stages of development – has increased substantially since 2016, peaking in 2024. Because these transactions are smaller than investments in later-stage companies, seed funding still makes up a small share of total VC investment but remains an important source of early-stage corporate funding (Figure 2.20, Panels A and B).

Figure 2.20. VC investment as a share of GDP

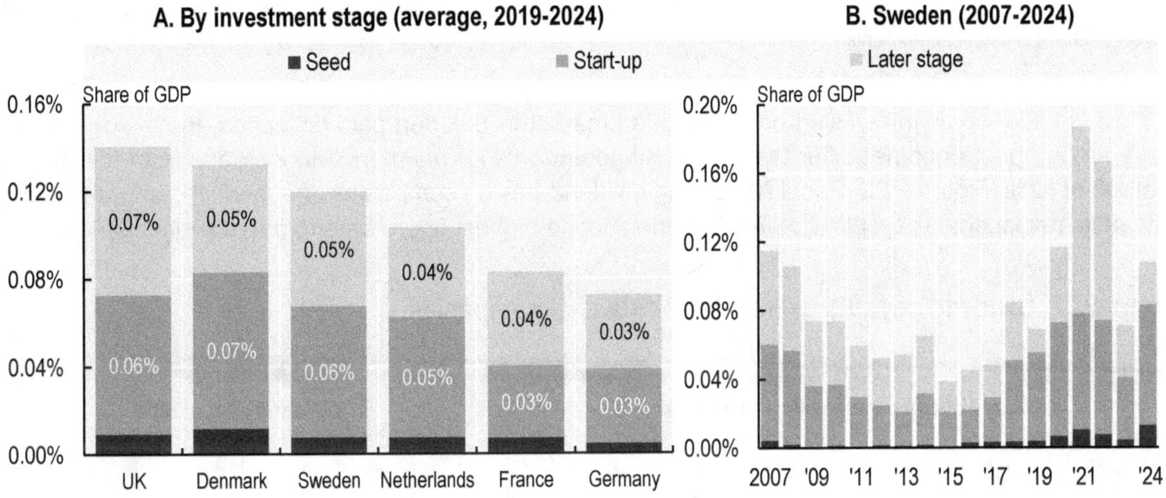

Note: By location of portfolio firm.
Source: OECD (2025[27]), Venture capital investments (market statistics), http://data-explorer.oecd.org/s/1o9

2.3. The corporate sector

2.3.1. Capital structure and performance

Equity financing accounts for over two-thirds of Swedish corporations' total funding, a level comparable to France and the United Kingdom, but well above the euro area figure of 58% (Figure 2.21, Panel A). A significant portion (70%) of this is in the form of unlisted shares. While the balance between listed and unlisted equity varies across countries, there has been a general shift towards unlisted equity financing over time, a trend driven in part by the growing availability of funding in private markets, which benefited from the low cost of debt in the aftermath of the 2008 financial crisis. The share of listed equity fell by 17 percentage points between 2005 and 2025 in the United Kingdom and by 7 percentage points in the euro area. In contrast, the share of listed equity in Sweden rose modestly from 29% to 30%. This increase was, however, smaller than in Denmark, where it grew by 4 percentage points over the same period.

Figure 2.21. Balance sheet composition, non-financial companies

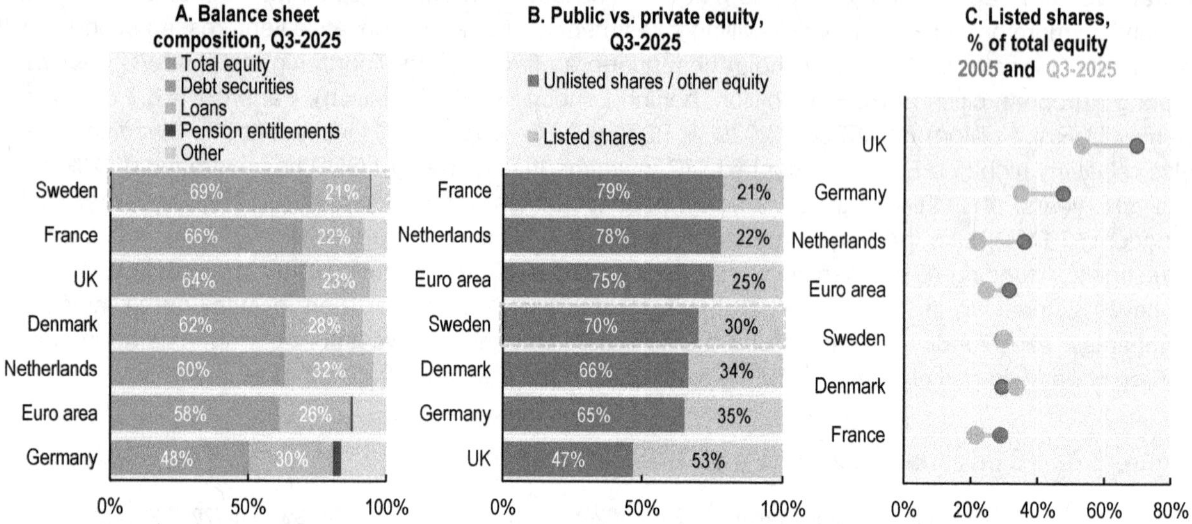

Source: ECB and ONS Sector Accounts.

In 2023, 61% of companies listed on a regulated market in Sweden paid dividends, the second highest share among peer countries after the United Kingdom (64%). This marks an increase from the 2005-15 average of 52% (Figure 2.22, Panel A). Among dividend-paying companies, the median company paid out 48% of its net income (payout ratio) in 2023, the second highest figure among peers (Panel B).

Figure 2.22. Dividend payouts by listed non-financial companies

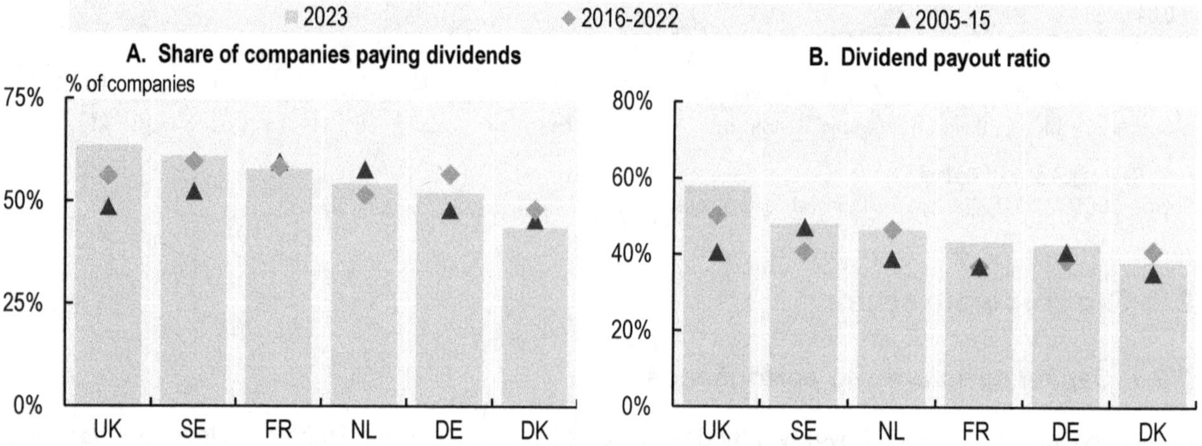

Note: Refers to companies listed on main markets. Panel B shows the ratio of dividends to net income, calculated for companies that have paid dividends and reported positive net income. The median value is computed for each year, and the average value is calculated based on the annual median values over the specified period.
Source: OECD Capital Market Series dataset, LSEG, see Annex for details.

Comparing companies listed on regulated markets and large unlisted firms (here defined as those with assets exceeding USD 100 million) can help identify potential barriers to accessing public markets. If a significant number of large, profitable companies remain unlisted, it is important from a policy perspective to assess whether regulatory constraints play a role. As shown in Figure 2.23, the revenue of the median listed Swedish company is more than twice that of the median large unlisted firm (USD 299 million versus USD 128 million) (Panel A). Since Swedish listed companies are already among the smallest in the peer group, however, there might not be significant untapped source of public market activity in the unlisted company universe. The difference in operating margins between listed and large unlisted companies in Sweden is among the largest observed in peer countries (Panel C). Even so, the 80th percentile of large unlisted companies generates revenues of USD 436 million, indicating at least some potential for further growth in the Swedish public equity market based on the existing universe of companies.

Figure 2.23. Median size and profitability of listed and large unlisted non-financial companies, 2023

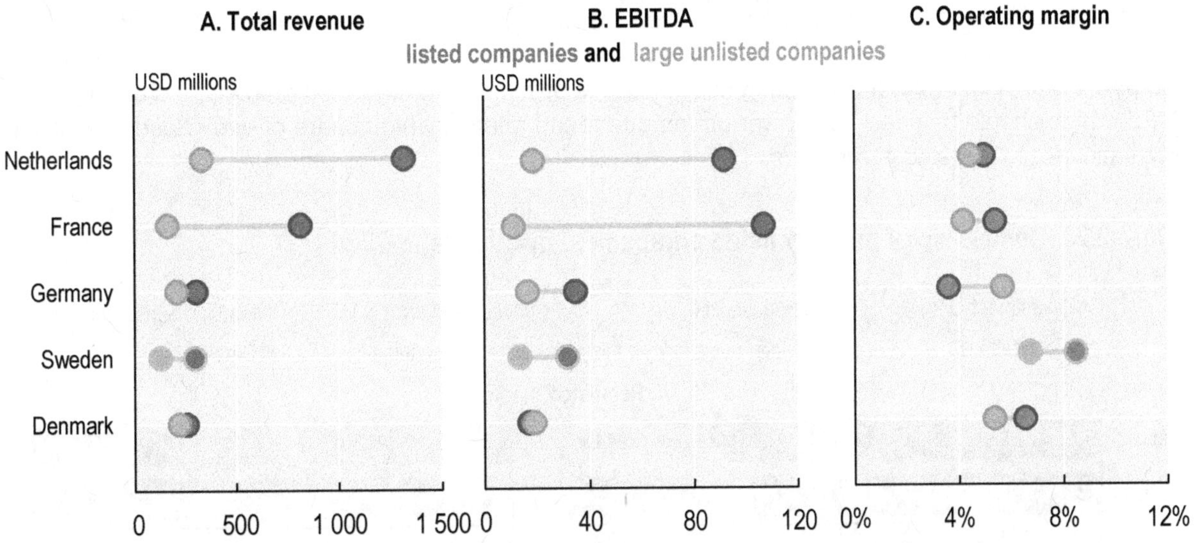

Note: Based on country of headquarters. Listed companies only include those listed on main markets. Large unlisted companies are defined as those with total assets exceeding USD 100 million. Operating margin is calculated as operating income divided by total sales.
Source: OECD Capital Market Series dataset, OECD-ORBIS Corporate Finance dataset, LSEG, see Annex for details.

There are, however, significant differences in balance sheet composition between large unlisted companies and listed companies in Sweden, with the latter tending to have significantly higher capitalisation levels. At the end of 2023, the median capitalisation of listed companies was 47%, compared to 32% for large unlisted companies, which instead rely more on long-term debt.

Figure 2.24. Capital structure, listed and large unlisted non-financial companies in Sweden

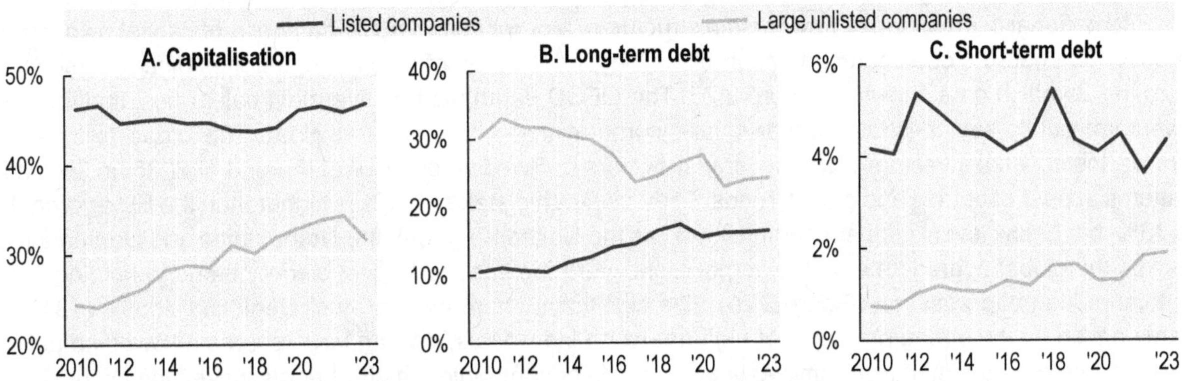

Source: OECD Capital Market Series dataset, OECD-ORBIS Corporate Finance dataset, LSEG, see Annex for details.

2.4. Investors and ownership structure

The Swedish public equity market is characterised by a significant presence of institutional investors (Figure 2.25). The level of investment fund ownership is particularly notable, although part of this refers to pension fund investments through funds (see Figure 2.37). At the end of 2024, traditional institutional investors – investment funds, pension funds and insurance companies – collectively owned more than half of all listed companies in Sweden. In terms of voting rights, however, their ownership is somewhat lower in regulated markets, due to investment firms/private equity and foundations wielding more voting power than their capital holdings would suggest, given the widespread use of dual class share structures in Sweden and the strong presence of strategic family owners (see Figure 2.30 and section 2.6). Households also play a significant role, representing nearly 15% of ownership in regulated markets and around 7% in MTFs, which should be seen as a lower bound due to the relatively high share of undisclosed ownership information for MTF-listed companies.

Figure 2.25. Ownership of publicly listed companies, Sweden, end-2024

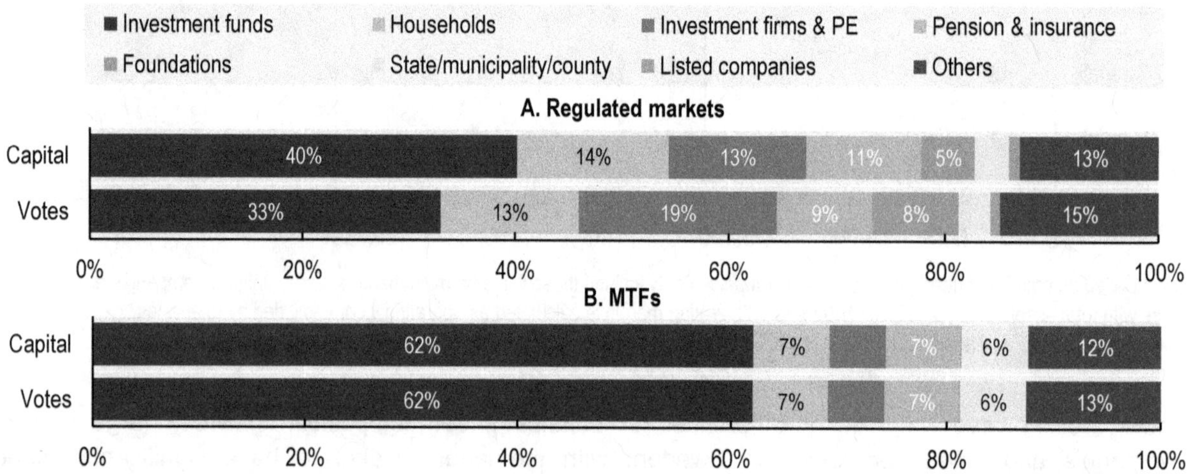

Note: Refers to shares of identified holdings. Unidentified holdings (typically where ownership shares are below regulatory thresholds) account for 12% of capital ownership in companies listed on regulated markets and 32% on MTFs. The "Others" category includes all owners that do not fall into any of the other seven categories, containing primarily corporate owners.
Source: Modular Finance Holdings database.

For international comparisons of ownership structures, a proprietary OECD database of capital ownership is used. To ensure cross-country comparability, the classification of investor categories differs somewhat from the Swedish data shown in Figure 2.25. The OECD database has five main categories: institutional investors; public sector; strategic individuals; corporations; and other free float. The broad trends are similar. Institutional investors were the largest owners of Swedish equities at the end of 2025, in line with patterns in peer countries and global trends. Their ownership stake of 37% is higher than the EU aggregate of 33%, but below levels in peer countries such as the United Kingdom, the Netherlands and Denmark, as well as the global aggregate of 47%. Corporations were the second-largest owner category, holding 14% of total market capitalisation (Figure 2.26). The significant share owned by strategic individuals (13%) is partly driven by the strong presence of high net-worth individuals, owning large shares of Swedish public equities through their stakes in family-owned investment companies, as further discussed in section 2.6.

Figure 2.26. Ownership of publicly listed companies, international comparison, end-2025

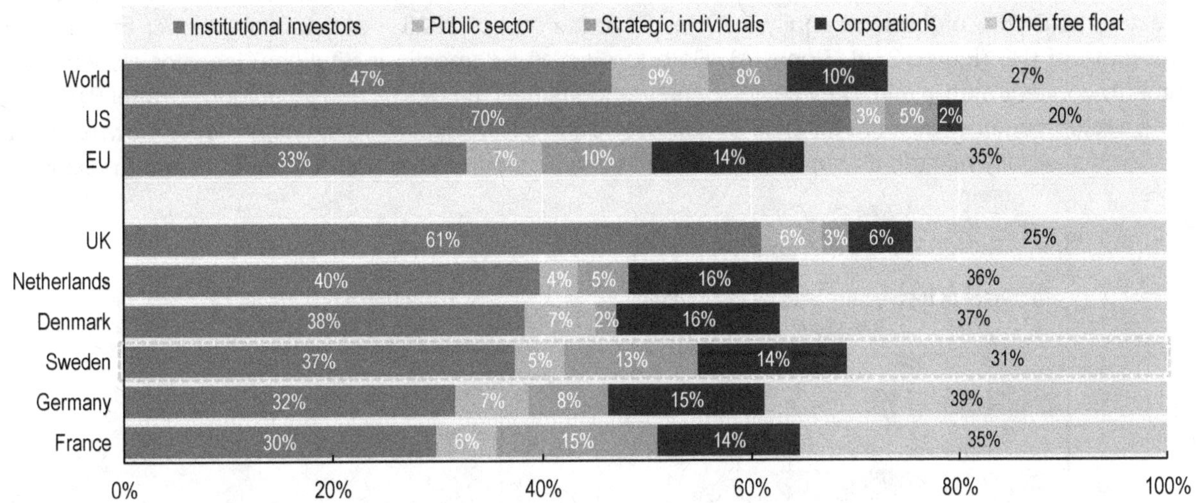

Note: Ongoing change of data providers means data may be subject to future revision, see Annex for details.
Source: OECD Capital Market Series dataset, FactSet, LSEG and Bloomberg; see Annex for details.

Domestic investors are prominent on the Swedish market, holding 45% of total public equity capital, the highest share among peer countries (Figure 2.27, Panel A). This can in large part be attributed to a set of large, domestically owned investment companies and a well-developed asset-backed pension system (see section 2.5). Direct household ownership is also widespread. Over 2 million people (nearly one-third of the adult population) own shares directly in a listed company, not including their ownership through investment companies or funds (Swedish Securities Market Association[28]). While foreign investors are naturally also significant, their share in total ownership is the lowest (24%) among the peer countries, and well below the EU aggregate of 35%. Notably, most of the foreign investor ownership in Sweden comes from institutional investors, accounting for 19% of market capitalisation and nearly 78% of total foreign ownership in the country (Panel B).

Figure 2.27. Ownership of public equity by origin and category of investors, end-2025

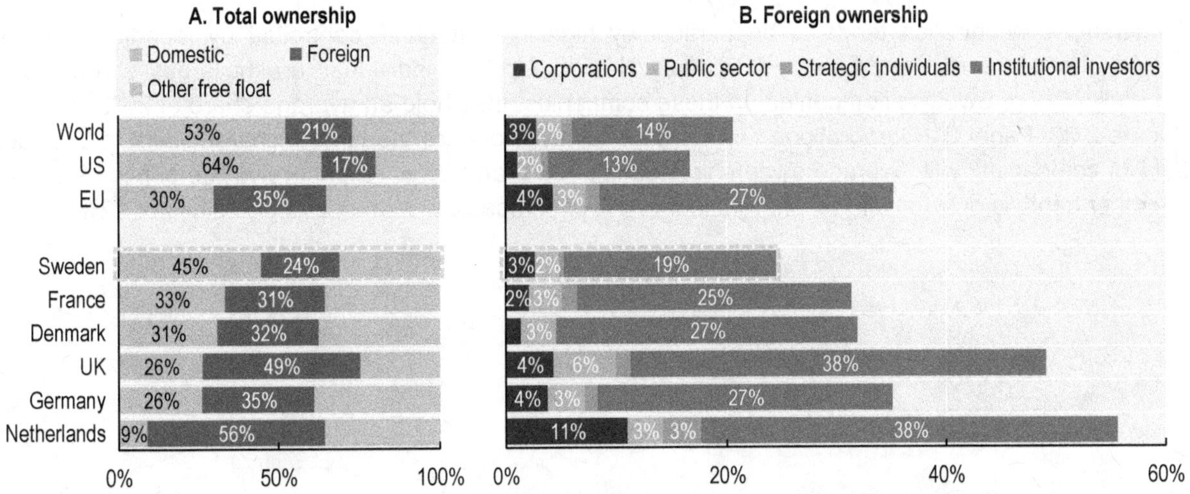

Note: The category "Other free float" in Panel A represents shares in the hands of investors that are not required to disclose their holdings and for which no information is therefore available. Ongoing change of data providers means data may be subject to future revision, see Annex for details.
Source: OECD Capital Market Series dataset, FactSet, LSEG and Bloomberg, see Annex for details.

Focusing on the largest investor category, institutional investors, about half of ownership in Sweden refers to international entities. This is significantly lower than in most peer countries. Domestic institutional investors held 18% of the total equity in Sweden at the end of 2025 – substantially higher than the EU aggregate of 6% (Figure 2.28, Panel A). Both foreign and domestic institutional investor ownership is primarily concentrated in a few key sectors, such as industrials, financials and technology (Panel B). These three sectors together account for 69% of domestic and 70% of foreign institutional investor ownership in the Swedish equity market, driven by large international companies such as Volvo, SEB and Ericsson.

Figure 2.28. Institutional investor ownership, end-2025

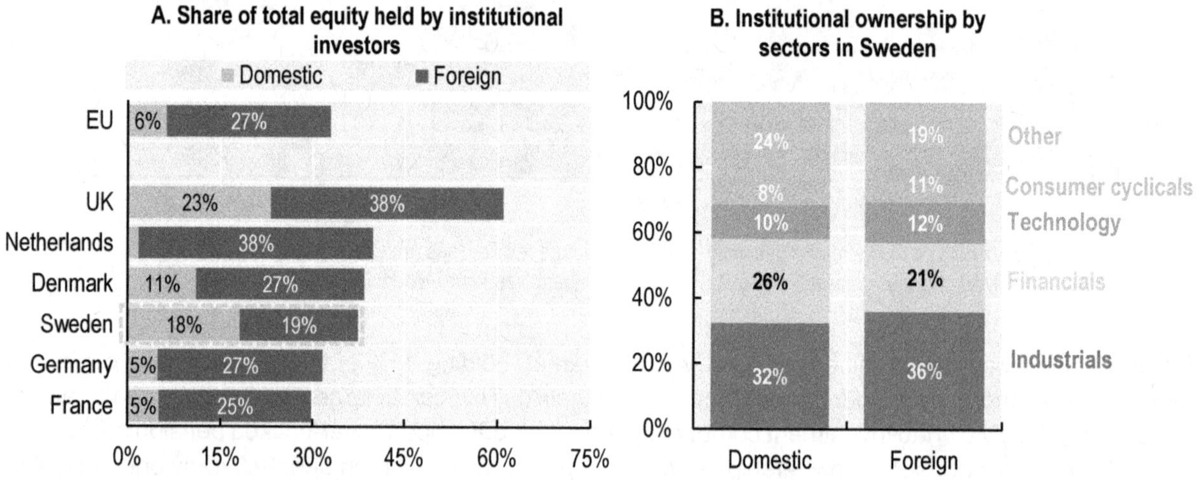

Note: Ongoing change of data providers means data may be subject to future revision, see Annex for details.
Source: OECD Capital Market Series dataset, FactSet, LSEG and Bloomberg, see Annex for details.

In terms of capital ownership, the Swedish equity market has a relatively dispersed ownership structure. In 2025, fewer than a quarter of companies had a major shareholder owning more than 30% of the equity – a markedly lower share than the EU average of 57% (Figure 2.29, Panel A). The same is not true when considering vote ownership, which is much more concentrated given the widespread use of dual class share structures (see Figure 2.30).

Ownership concentration tends to be particularly high in companies controlled by founding families, individual entrepreneurs and wealthy individuals. Notably, strategic individuals are the largest shareholders in nearly 40% of Swedish companies. In these companies, they hold an average share of 26% of capital (Figure 2.29, Panel B). Corporations and institutional investors are the largest shareholders in 38% and 21% of companies, with average ownership stakes of 22% and 20%, respectively. The public sector, on the other hand, is only the largest shareholder in 1% of companies, with an average stake of 12%.

Figure 2.29. Ownership concentration, end-2025

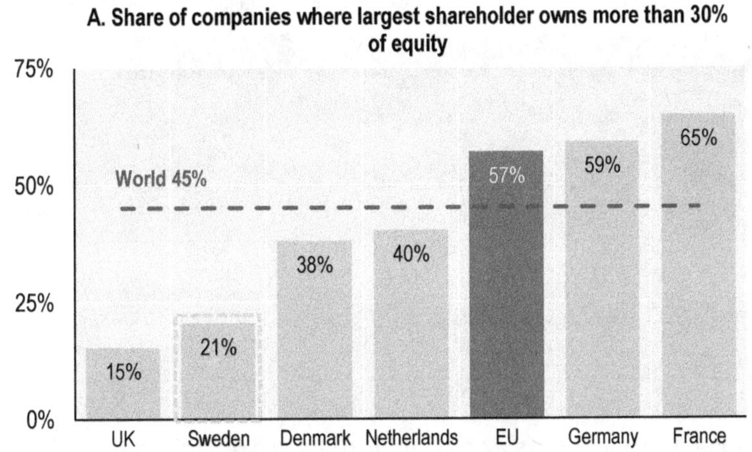

B. Largest shareholder category, Sweden

Shareholder category	Largest owner in % of companies	Avg. ownership in these companies
Strategic individuals	39%	26%
Corporations	38%	22%
Institutional investors	21%	20%
Public sector	1%	12%

Note: Panel B shows the share of companies where each investor category is the largest shareholder, and the average share of equity held by that category in those companies. For example, strategic individuals are the largest shareholder in 39% of companies; in these companies, strategic individuals own an average of 26% of the equity. Ongoing change of data providers means data may be subject to future revision, see Annex for details.
Source: OECD Capital Market Series dataset, FactSet, LSEG and Bloomberg, see Annex for details.

Dual-class share (DCS) structures, granting certain shareholders higher voting rights compared to their equity ownership, have been present in the Swedish corporate landscape for over a century. By the end of 2025, 49% of companies listed on the regulated markets had DCS structures, representing almost three-quarters of the total market capitalisation (Figure 2.30). This is among the highest share in Europe (ISS, 2023[29]). DCS are less prevalent on MTFs, corresponding to 26% of market capitalisation.

Business organisations generally see DCS structures as well-functioning in Sweden, arguing it contributes to a stable and long-term investor base that allows companies to adopt a strategic, long-term operational outlook (Confederation of Swedish Enterprise, 2023[30]). The domestic model of active family ownership notably relies in large part on the use of DCS structures. Since 1945, Swedish law allows for a maximum 1 to 10 voting ratio between the weakest and strongest voting shares (prior to this there was no upper limit).

The disproportionate control granted by DCS is however a subject of discussion elsewhere, notably in continental Europe, sometimes raising concerns regarding for example minority shareholder protection and potential misalignment of interests. Countries adopt varying approaches to DCS, some allowing different degrees of voting rights per share, others requiring companies to seek shareholder approval after a certain period to retain them (Pereira, 2023[31]). Box 2.4 provides a summary of how these issues are balanced in Swedish regulation. Given different regulations across EU countries, the European Commission proposed a new directive in December 2022 aiming to facilitate the listing of SMEs with provisions on how they can adopt DCS structures, as a way to encourage founders to access capital markets while retaining control of the company (European Commission, 2022[32]). In 2023, the European Council adopted a negotiating mandate on this proposed directive which was formally adopted in late 2024. After entering into force, member states have two years to adopt the legal and administrative provisions necessary to comply with this directive.

Figure 2.30. Share of Swedish listed companies with dual class share structures, end-2025

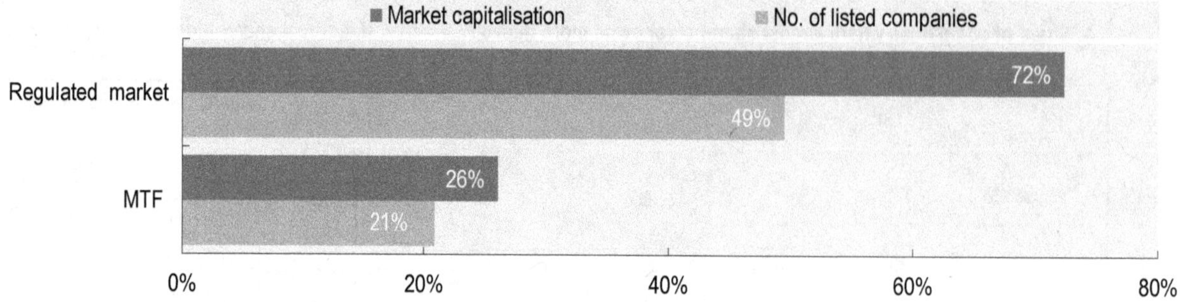

Source: Bloomberg, OECD Capital Market Series dataset, LSEG; see Annex for details.

Box 2.4. Shareholder control, dual class shares and balancing majority/minority interests

The Swedish corporate governance model is almost entirely hierarchical; management is completely controlled by the board of directors, and the board of directors is in turn controlled by the general shareholder meeting, which for most intents and purposes has unrestricted legal competence to decide on any matter concerning the company, including at a detailed business level. To ensure that the board elected by shareholders is not in effect controlled by management, the Swedish Corporate Governance Code requires not only that the board is elected by the general shareholder meeting, but also that it is proposed by a nomination committee consisting of shareholder representatives, appointed by shareholders at the general meeting. This implies that a shareholder with practical majority control of the votes in the company can exert significant control, but also that efficient governance requires there to be a shareholder, or a coalition of shareholders, that monitors the company, engages with the board, and proposes and votes on important matters such as the election of board directors. Dual class share structures have been allowed in Swedish law for over a century to facilitate such engagement. Since the 1940s, shareholders have been allowed to adopt a voting structure where one share class has up to 10 times the votes of the weakest share class.

The most prominent challenge in a system built on shareholder control is the risk of the controlling shareholder abusing minority shareholders. To mitigate this risk, Swedish corporate law provides a very extensive framework for minority protection (Lekvall, 2014[33]; Gilson, 2014[34]; Nenova, 2003[4]), consisting of, among other things:

- **Equal treatment of shareholders**: A general prohibition on any decision by the general shareholder meeting or actions by the company that in practice leads to unequal treatment of shareholders.
- **Individual shareholder rights:** Extensive individual shareholder rights, allowing any shareholder (regardless of the size of their holdings) to add items to the agenda of the general shareholder meeting, to ask the board questions at the general shareholder meeting, and to challenge a decision by the general shareholder meeting in court (with the court being able to invalidate a decision and even replace it with another).
- **Shareholder rights for significant minority shareholders:** A shareholder or a group of shareholders holding more than 10 per cent of the shares in a company can demand that an extraordinary general shareholder meeting be held, that a special accountant is elected to ensure that minority interests are considered in the audit, that a legal review is carried out to investigate if any particular event in the company complies with corporate law, and even that minimum dividends are paid.

- **Majority vote requirements:** For most major general shareholder meeting decisions except the election of the board, the Swedish Companies Act requires that the decision be approved by a qualified majority, ranging from two-thirds to total unanimity. In these cases, both votes and capital are counted, ensuring that a DCS structure does not allow a majority shareholder to dominate important corporate decisions.

2.5. Institutional investors

2.5.1. Pension funds

Pension funds and capital markets have a symbiotic relationship. Investing in global capital markets helps ensure the solvency of asset-backed pension systems, contributing to better retirement outcomes for pensioners. At the same time, when they are sizeable, pension funds also contribute to the development of capital markets (Babalos and Stavroyiannis, 2020[35]; Niggemann and Rocholl, 2010[36]). Pension funds can thereby provide dual benefits to the real economy, directly by financing corporate and sovereign investment, and indirectly by laying the foundations for access to other funding by increasing the depth of capital markets. Establishing a well-functioning channel between pension funds and capital markets is therefore a key policy concern. Unlike the United States, where pension fund assets total over 150% of GDP (US Federal Reserve, 2026[37]) sizeable asset-backed pension funds are relatively rare in Europe. Instead, most European countries rely to very large extent on pay-as-you-go models where pension disbursements are funded by taxes (or levies/fees) on the current working population. Sweden is an exception to this norm. Household pension entitlements amount to 300% of GDP, over a third of which (109% of GDP) is funded. It is one of only three EU countries with a sizeable share of funded entitlements, together with the Netherlands where almost half of entitlements are funded and Denmark where about three quarters are funded. Sweden's share in aggregate EU pension fund assets is more than seven times higher than its GDP share would suggest (Figure 2.31, Panels A and B). This gives Swedish capital markets access to a significant source of domestic funding.

Figure 2.31. Funded and unfunded pension entitlements

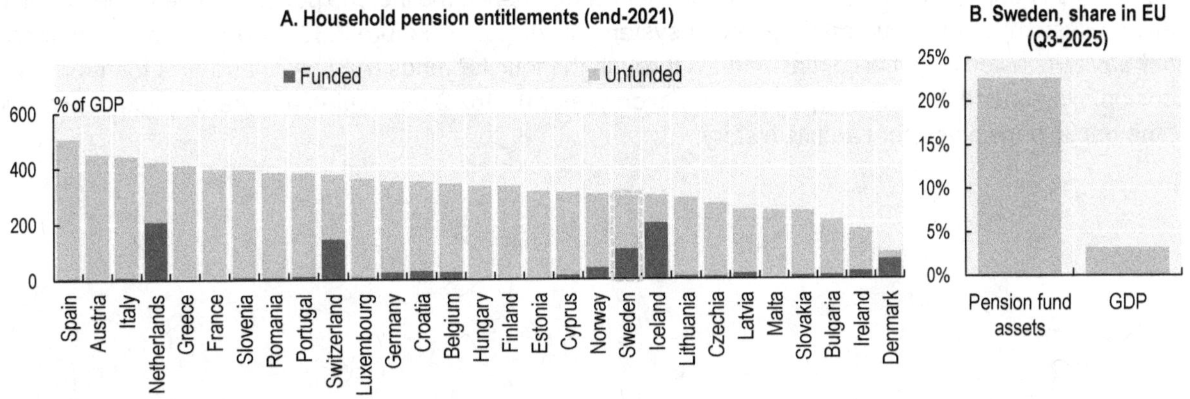

Note: Data not available for Poland.
Source: Eurostat, ECB.

While the Swedish funded pension system has developed over a long time, most of the growth in assets under management is relatively recent. Total assets in the pension system, including public, occupational and certain earmarked private assets, have grown by 178% since the 2008 financial crisis, reaching a total of SEK 10.1 trillion (EUR 884 billion) at the end of 2024 (Figure 2.32). Over half of this growth came from increases in occupational pension fund assets, but the assets under management in the public pension system are also significant. Together, these two systems represent 96% of earmarked pension assets in Sweden. They are described in turn below. It bears noting that private savings invested in capital markets that are not earmarked for pension savings (such as through ISK accounts) are also significant in Sweden – these are addressed further under section 2.7 dealing with household savings. It should also be emphasised that the distribution of assets under management does not reflect average pension disbursements for retirees – public pensions represented nearly 70% of average pension disbursements in 2024 (Swedish Pensions Agency, 2026[38]).

Figure 2.32. Assets under management in the Swedish pension system

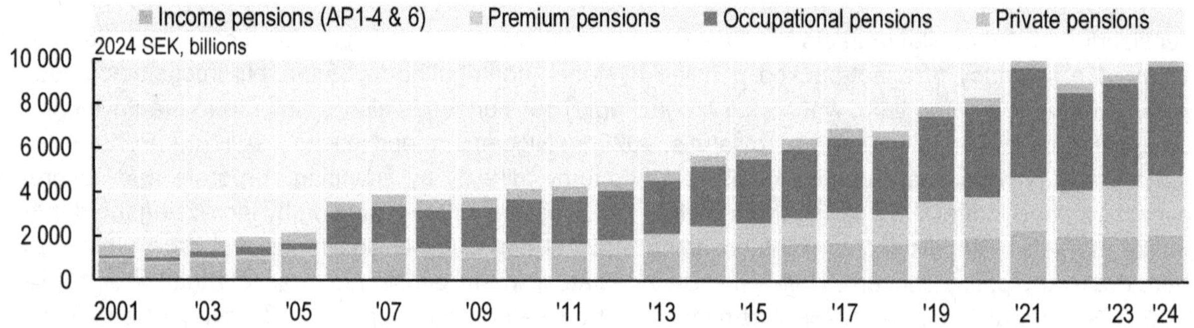

Note: Refers only to actual investment assets, excludes future contribution assets. Assets in the income pension system refer to the total assets under management of AP1-4 and AP6. Note that these were restructured and merged into three funds at the end of 2025 (see Box 2.5). Assets in the premium system include AP7 and all private funds. Occupational pension assets refer to those managed by life insurance firms and dedicated occupational pension companies (reported as an aggregate figure until 2021). Private pensions include private pension savings through life insurance companies and occupational pension companies. Other individual pension accounts (like IPS, for which statistics have been discontinued since 2019) are not included. Inflation adjustment is done using CPIF inflation (excluding household interest costs on housing).
Source: Swedish Pension Agency annual reports, AP funds' annual reports, Insurance Sweden.

The public pension system

The Swedish public pension system has three main components: the income pension system, the premium pension system and the guarantee pension system, illustrated in Figure 2.33. The first two components are heavily invested in global capital markets through the four AP funds (AP2, AP3 and AP4 for the income pension system and AP7 for the premium pension system). Box 2.5 provides a more detailed description of the public pension system and its history.

Figure 2.33. The Swedish public pension system

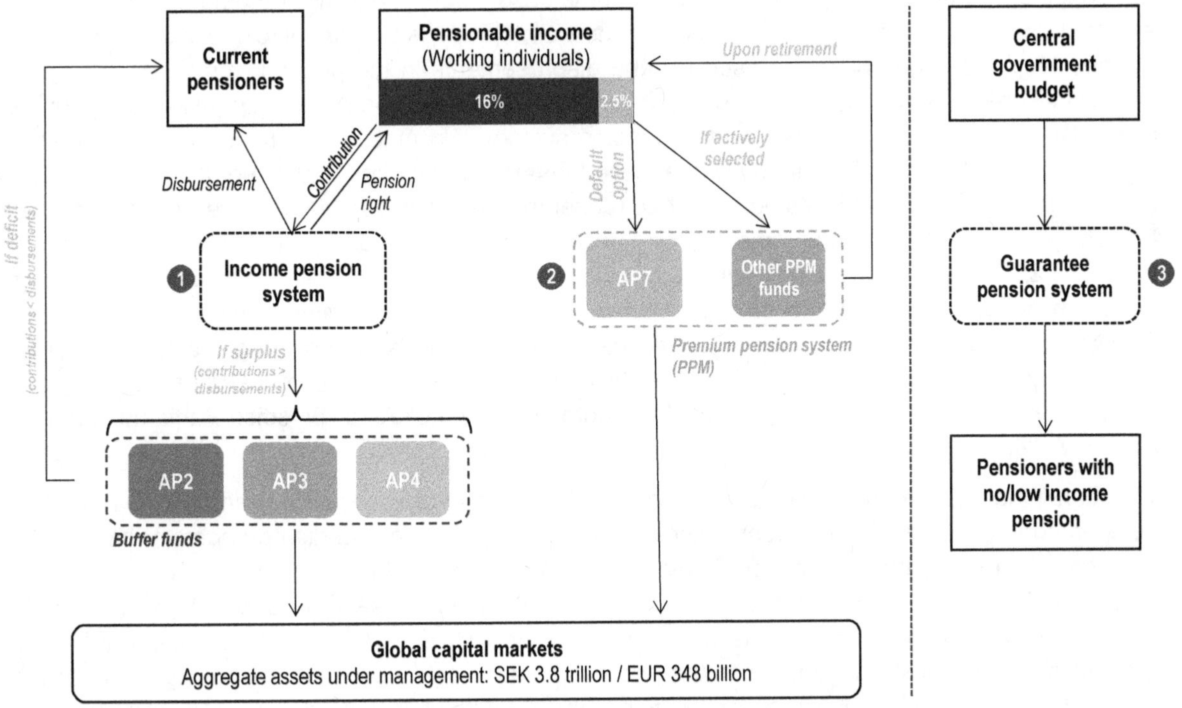

Box 2.5. The structure of the public pension system

The original Swedish public pension system, established in 1913, was the world's first near-universal social security system. It had two main components: a fee-based pension based on individual taxable income and a means-tested supplementary pension funded by general taxes (Edebalk, 2013[39]). The system has since then undergone two major reforms that saw it become increasingly connected to capital markets. The first was the introduction in 1960 of a general supplementary pension (*allmän tilläggspension*, ATP) funded by mandatory contributions by employers and employees on top of the basic public pension that had been established in 1948. The ATP system tied pensioners' benefits to their income and number of working years, meaning it effectively transformed the view of pensions in Sweden from a state allowance to a deferred salary (Swedish Pension Agency[40]). As part of this reform, three public pension funds – the first, second and third AP funds – were established to safeguard the solvency of the pension system. These funds were restricted to investing in fixed income securities. This changed in 1974 with the creation of the fourth AP fund, which was the first fund that was eligible to invest in Swedish public equities (AP2[41]). In other words, Swedish wage-earners have had a stake in domestic equity market development through the pension system for half a century.

In the ATP system, disbursements were tied to a price index. This led to a growing disconnect from real economic developments when economic growth stalled. Coupled with increases in life expectancy, also not accounted for, this threatened the financial solvency of the system. A second major reform was therefore initiated to replace the ATP system in the 1980s, eventually resulting in today's framework, which has been operational since 2003. It applies to the vast majority of the population; the old ATP system applies fully only to people born before 1938 with transition measures for those born between then and 1953 (Regeringskansliet, 2020[42]). The current public pension system, illustrated in Figure 2.33, has three main components and is largely independent from the central government budget.

The largest component is the income pension system. Each year, 18.5% of working individuals' pensionable income, up to a maximum of 7.5 income base amounts (IBA) is withheld. IBA is an inflation adjusted measure used to calculate the income pension; 7.5 IBA is equivalent to c. EUR 57 500 in 2026. Of this, 16 percentage points are used to fund disbursements in the public income pension system (Swedish Pension Agency[43]). These contributions give individuals proportional pension rights for their own retirement, effectively a claim on the pension system. If contributions exceed disbursements on aggregate in the system, the surplus is channelled in three equal parts to three of the AP buffer funds (AP2-4) and subsequently invested in global capital markets. Conversely, if there is a deficit, this is funded in equal parts by disbursements from these buffer funds (AP2[44]). Today, there are four main funds, AP2, AP3, AP4 and AP7 (the funds have been renumbered and reformed over time). The first three are buffer funds for the income pension system (Swedish Parliament, 2020[45]). This structure follows a 2025 government decision to consolidate the buffer funds through mergers, where AP1 was incorporated into AP3 and AP4, and AP6 – which was a closed-end fund focused entirely on private equity investment – was incorporated into AP2, both at the end of 2025 (Swedish Parliament, 2025[46]; AP4[47]; AP2[48]).

The remaining 2.5 percentage points are allocated to the premium pension system. Unlike the income pension contributions, premium pension contributions are paid into a dedicated account belonging to the individual making the contribution. They are therefore a type of mandatory private pension savings (and classified as such in the national accounts). The default option is for this capital to be managed by the state-run AP7 fund, which consists of an equity fund and a fixed income fund (the allocation between them shifts automatically depending on the account holder's age, becoming increasingly conservative as people near retirement). However, in addition to the default option, individuals are also free to choose from a large range of privately managed funds (currently nearly 400). There are no fees for switching funds, nor any limitations on the number of switches allowed (Swedish Pension Agency[49]). Individuals can start drawing from both the income and premium pensions from the age of 63 (Swedish Pension Agency[50]).

The third and final component of the public pension system is the guarantee pension system, which secures a minimum pension level for people with no or low income pensions. This component is financed through the central government budget.

The following section describes the AP fund structure as it stood before the restructuring effective from 2026. In the fourth quarter of 2025, the six – since merged to four – AP funds managed a total of SEK 3.8 trillion (c. EUR 348 billion). This corresponds to 18% of total public pension assets, with the remainder referring to total contribution assets, i.e. future pension contributions (AP2[44]). AP7, the premium pension system fund, is by far the largest, representing about 41% of total AP assets. Around half of total assets in the premium pension system are managed by AP7. The other half is managed by different private funds (Swedish Pension Agency, 2024[51]). The four (since 2026 merged to three) main buffer funds are roughly equal in size, while the PE-focused AP6 (now part of AP2) is significantly smaller. AP7 has historically used leverage to boost returns. It currently maintains a leverage level of approximately 25%, achieved through investments in derivative securities (AP7[52]).

Perhaps the most notable feature of the Swedish public pension system is the high allocation to equities. The buffer funds are all allowed to invest in a mixed portfolio, both with respect to asset classes and geographic exposure. Among them, public equity as a share of total assets under management (AUM) ranges from 42% to 57%. Of this, between a quarter and a third represents domestic equities. This gives Swedish companies access to a significant pool of long-term institutional investor capital, providing an advantage, all else equal, compared to countries with lower shares of funded pensions and with less capital market-oriented pension funds. Pension fund involvement in domestic equity markets is not limited to the regulated markets. AP1, AP2 and AP4 all directly hold shares listed on the main local growth market

(Nasdaq First North) as well. However, restrictions with respect to maximum allowed levels of ownership in individual companies, coupled with the relatively smaller size of MTF companies, serve to limit widespread MTF investment by pension funds. AP1 to 4 (since 2026 AP2 to 4) are not allowed to hold shares or other participations in a company that would give them more than 10% of total voting rights (Act (2000:192)[53]). Pension fund investment on MTFs is therefore restricted to the largest companies. Nevertheless, their engagement lends a legitimacy to these markets that contributes to a capital market ecosystem that encourages smaller companies to go public, as is evident from the large number of companies listed on Swedish growth markets (see section 2.1.6).

Numerous factors have contributed to the significant allocation of assets to domestic equities. One is simply the attractive historical returns of the Swedish equity market (see section 2.1.1). The domestic corporate governance model's strong focus on shareholder control, notably through nomination committees (see Box 2.4), is also important since it allows large investors like pension funds significant influence in corporate governance and management decisions, reducing the perceived investment risk of equities. Another aspect that may have contributed is the regulation that the AP funds are subject to with respect to foreign currency exposure. By law, no more than 40% of each fund's assets can be subject to currency risk (Act (2000:192)[53]). This means that at least 60% of the funds' assets must be invested in instruments denominated in Swedish krona or hedged to mitigate currency risk. The requirement has, however, been a topic of discussion, especially following periods of significant exchange rate movements. For example, in 2022, the Swedish krona depreciated significantly against major currencies, which could have positively influenced the funds' returns if not for the mandatory currency hedging. An industry report has noted that these legal restrictions on currency exposure limit the potential benefits from such currency movements and recommended that the government reevaluate this policy (Investment & Pensions Europe, 2023[54]). Moreover, the funds themselves have indicated that these regulations impose liquidity constraints (AP6, 2024[55]).

Figure 2.34. Overview of the AP funds (public pension funds), Q4-2025

	Assets under management (SEKbn)	Investment strategy	Public equity, % of AUM	Domestic equity, % of total public equity holdings
AP1 (buffer)	520	Mixed, global	56%	34%
AP2 (buffer)	475	Mixed, global	42%	25%
AP3 (buffer)	577	Mixed, global	49%	26%
AP4 (buffer)	578	Mixed, global	57%	26%
AP6 (buffer)	84	Private equity, global	n.a.	n.a.
AP7 (premium)	1,529	Equity/fixed income	86%	1%

Note: Refers to AP buffer fund structure as of end-2025 – note that these funds were restructured and merged into three funds at the end of 2025 (see Box 2.5). Public equity exposure is based on funds' disclosed allocation by asset class and includes potential exposure through investment funds. Domestic equity shares have been calculated based on direct holdings where available. AP4 equity holdings include "defensive equities" (c. 7% of total equity holdings) which have not been classified according to geography. AP6 has no public equity data since it focuses on private equity. For AP7, public equity as a share of AUM is calculated by dividing the value of the AP7 Equity Fund's public equity holdings by the combined total AUM of the AP7 Equity Fund and the AP7 Fixed Income Fund.
Source: Fund holdings and annual reports.

The focus on equities is also clear in the pension system more broadly. Figure 2.35 compares the share of equities in total financial assets for all pension funds (not just public ones) in European peer countries. Sweden and Denmark stand out due to the high direct allocations to equity. Nearly a quarter of the assets in the Swedish pension system are direct equity holdings (of which 72% is publicly listed securities) – more than one and a half times the euro area aggregate. In addition, over half of Swedish pension funds' total assets are held in investment fund shares for which look-through data are not available for international comparison. Based on the public AP funds' portfolios and direct and indirect (look-through) exposure of occupational pension funds (see Figure 2.37), total equity exposure by Swedish pension funds is likely to be significantly higher due to their holdings of investment fund shares.

Figure 2.35. Pension funds' direct equity and investment fund share holdings, Q3-2025

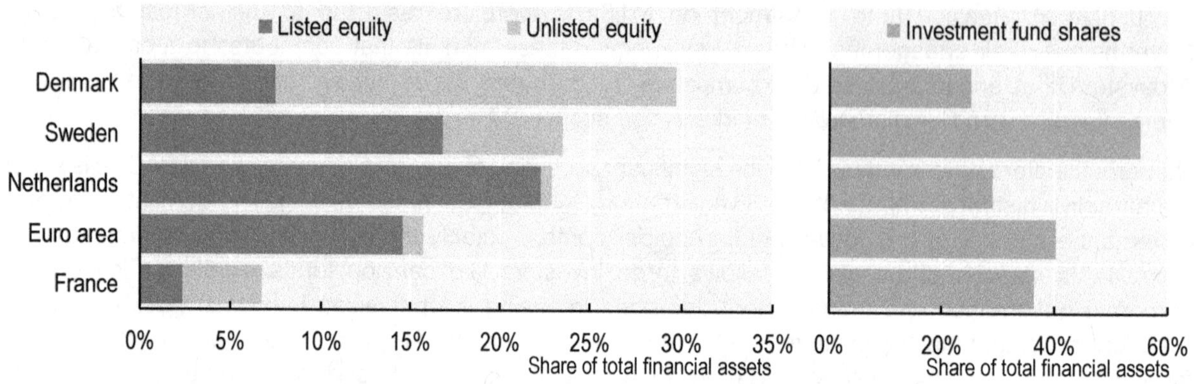

Note: Equity holdings refer only to direct holdings, not holdings through collective investment undertakings. For international comparability, pension funds are here defined in line with sector S129 in the 2010 European System of Accounts (ESA 2010), which excludes buffer funds, and is not restricted to public funds. Following this definition, Swedish pension funds' total assets amounted to SEK 8.7 trillion (EUR 801 billion) in Q3-2025.
Source: ECB.

The occupational pension system

Sweden has long had an extensive occupational pension system. Its establishment was the key ambition that drove the introduction of the ATP system in 1960. Today, over 90% of Swedish employees are covered by a semi-mandatory occupational pension scheme (Regeringskansliet, 2020[42]). Given the scope of the Swedish occupational pension system, fund assets are very substantial, representing 49% of total pension fund assets, the largest component of the pension system (Figure 2.32). However, for the average earner the mandatory public pension remains the most important. Mandatory private schemes represent around a fifth of the Swedish gross replacement rate (pension benefits at retirement relative to earnings when working) of 64% (Figure 2.36).

Figure 2.36. Gross replacement rate of mandatory schemes, 2025

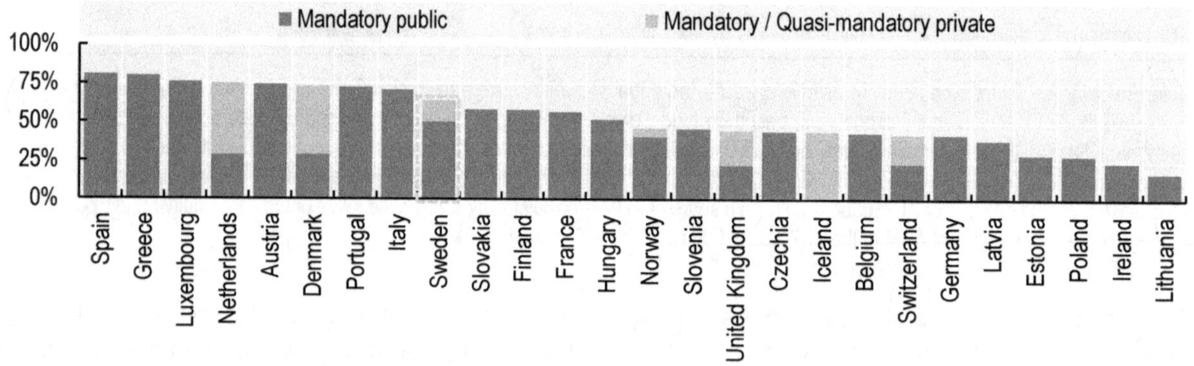

Note: Shows the replacement rate of the average earner. Quasi-mandatory schemes are the ones covering at least 85% of employees. Such schemes exist in Denmark, the Netherlands, Sweden and the United Kingdom.
Source: OECD (2025[56]) Pensions at a Glance 2025: OECD and G20 Indicators, https://www.oecd.org/en/publications/pensions-at-a-glance-2025_e40274c1-en.html.

Box 2.6. The structure of the occupational pension system

Like the public pension system, the occupational system has moved from a defined benefit towards a defined contribution model over time. All employment that is governed by a collective agreement between unions and employers' confederations (roughly 90% of Swedish employees) includes occupational pension coverage. There are different schemes depending on employment type; those with white collar employment under collective agreement in the private sector are covered by a specific scheme called ITP, negotiated between the Swedish trade union association PTK and the Confederation of Swedish Enterprise. Similar to the public premium pension fund AP7, while there is a default fund choice for the management of the ITP pension, it is also possible for individuals to choose among a number of funds and investment strategies. The contributions to these schemes typically range between 4.5 and 6 per cent of the monthly salary, up to 7.5 income base amounts annually (equivalent to a monthly salary of SEK 52 125 or EUR 4 820). For income above this amount, a much higher contribution of between 30-31.5 per cent is applied (Collectum[57]; Konsumenternas[58]).

Similar to the asset-backed part of the public pension system, occupational pension funds in Sweden have a much more equity-focused investment approach than those in peer countries. Total equity exposure represents almost half of the aggregate portfolio. The majority of this refers to direct holdings of listed equities (36%), followed by unlisted equities (7%) and indirect equity exposure through investment funds (5%). Total equity exposure is 9 percentage points higher than in the Netherlands, the second most equity-intensive market, and as much as 40 percentage points higher than in Germany. This allocation has contributed to sustained growth in total assets over time – as of the third quarter of 2025, total Swedish occupational pension fund investment assets were larger in absolute euro terms than those in France and Germany, economies that are more than five and seven times larger, respectively (Figure 2.37).

Figure 2.37. Occupational pension funds' asset exposures, Q3-2025

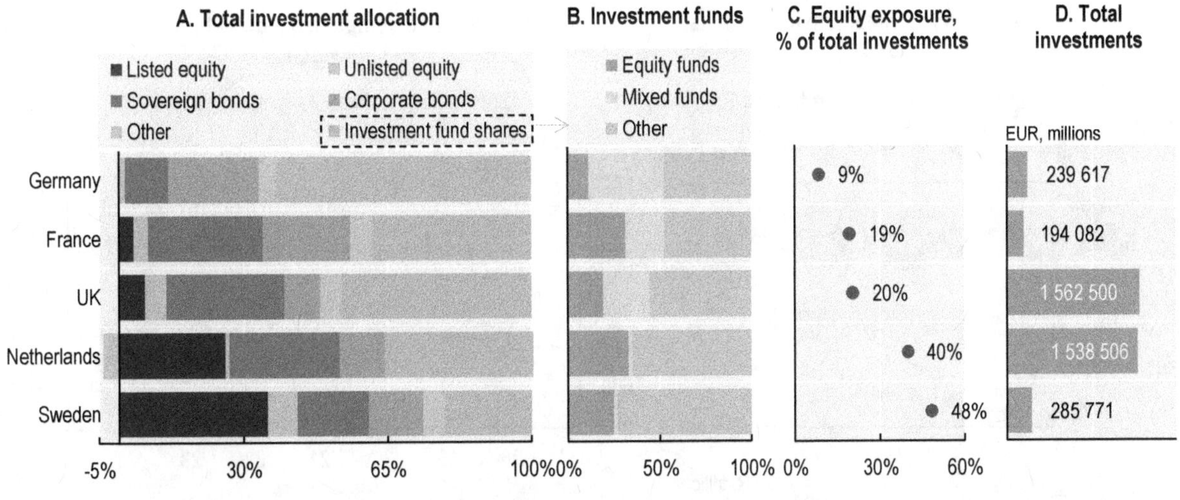

Note: Data not available for Denmark. UK data refer to Q1-2025. Panel A shows shares of total investments. Derivatives exposure is negative in the Netherlands. Panel B shows shares of total investment fund investments. Panel C includes direct investments in listed and unlisted equity as well as indirect investments through equity funds (excluding mixed funds).
Source: EIOPA IORP statistics, Office for National Statistics (ONS).

2.5.2. Insurance companies

Insurance companies help stabilise economic conditions for households and corporations, influencing their capacity and willingness to invest. Beyond their role in enabling risk-sharing they are, like pension funds, key participants in capital markets themselves, providing long-term financing to corporations and governments alike.

The insurance market is typically divided into two main subsectors: life and non-life insurance. Life insurance covers financial risks related to the death of the insured, providing payments to one or more designated beneficiaries. Non-life insurance, on the other hand, includes various policies that protect against risks such as property damage, health issues, and accidents, offering financial compensation for unexpected events. Investment strategies differ across these segments. While non-life insurance companies invest in shorter-duration assets to manage frequent claims payments, life insurance companies focus on longer-term investments aligned with the extended timelines of the payouts (Svensk Försäkring, 2025[59]). In Sweden, the insurance industry consists of 31 life insurance companies, 202 non-life insurance companies and 20 mutual benefit associations.[2] The industry is highly concentrated, with a few firms dominating the market. Despite the smaller number of life insurance companies compared to non-life companies, the former group manages significantly more assets.

As of the third quarter of 2025, Swedish insurance companies (excluding occupational retirement provisions of life insurance undertakings) managed assets equivalent to 73% of the country's GDP, roughly in the middle of the distribution among peer countries (Figure 2.38, Panel A). Despite restrictions on portfolio composition (see Box 2.7), Swedish insurance companies, like pension funds, maintain substantial exposure to equity markets. Their combined direct equity holdings and indirect exposure through investments in equity funds grew from SEK 1 197 billion in 2017 to SEK 2 595 billion in the third quarter of 2025. Equity holdings by insurance companies have also grown as a share of GDP, particularly from 2018 to 2021 when it peaked at 41% (Panel B).

Figure 2.38. Insurance companies' asset exposures

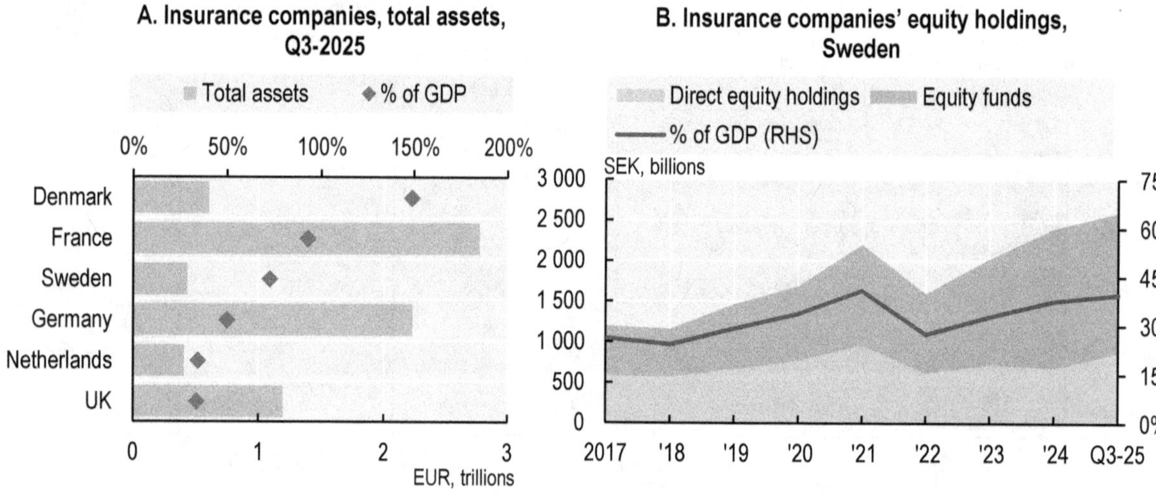

Source: EIOPA, Bank of England, Eurostat, OECD. Data covers insurance groups reporting under Solvency II.

High levels of equity investment are evident when looking at the portfolio composition of Swedish insurance companies. The largest share of their investment assets (62% as of the third quarter of 2025) is allocated to investment funds, a proportion significantly higher than that of their international peers (Figure 2.39, Panel A). Notably, equity funds dominate this category, accounting for 58% of the total, also the highest share among peer countries (Panel B). While direct equity investments are smaller, they still represent nearly a fifth of total assets. In contrast, investments in debt (including direct holdings of corporate and sovereign bonds as well as debt funds) make up the smallest share of Swedish insurance companies' investment assets.

Figure 2.39. Insurance companies' asset allocation, Q3-2025

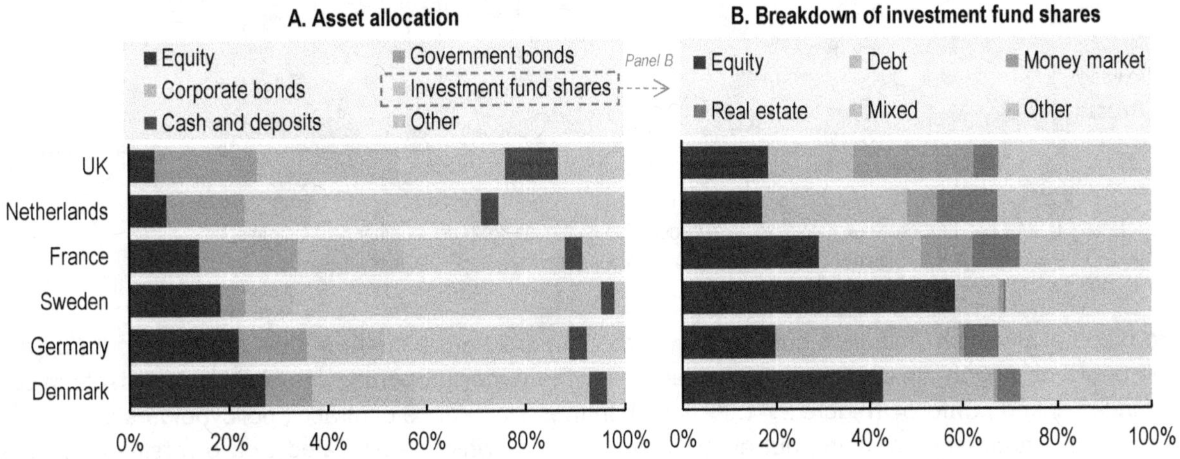

Note: Data covers insurance groups reporting under Solvency II.
Source: OECD, EIOPA, Bank of England.

Overall, Swedish insurance companies have by far the highest total equity allocation (direct and indirect) among peer countries. As of the third quarter of 2025, equity accounted for 55% of total assets, far exceeding peer countries such as France (24%), the Netherlands (13%) and the United Kingdom (9%). In contrast, Swedish insurance companies have the lowest allocation to government debt, representing just 5% of total assets, compared to an average of 16% among its peers (Figure 2.40, Panel A). This limited investment in sovereign debt partly reflects a low level of Swedish government debt, which at the end of 2023 amounted to the lowest share of GDP recorded since the mid-1960s for the central government (Riksgälden, 2024[60]). Representatives of the Swedish Debt Office have noted that "excessively low" government debt can pose challenges with respect to market liquidity, undermining the role of government securities as a safe asset and thereby complicating their use as a risk-free benchmark, with implications for pricing and hedging in other markets (Bjellerup and Rådahl, 2023[61]). Among Swedish insurance companies' total bond investments, government bonds constituted only 34%, with Denmark being the only peer country where insurance companies allocate a smaller share of assets to government debt (Panel B).

Figure 2.40. Insurance companies' equity and government debt exposure, Q3-2025

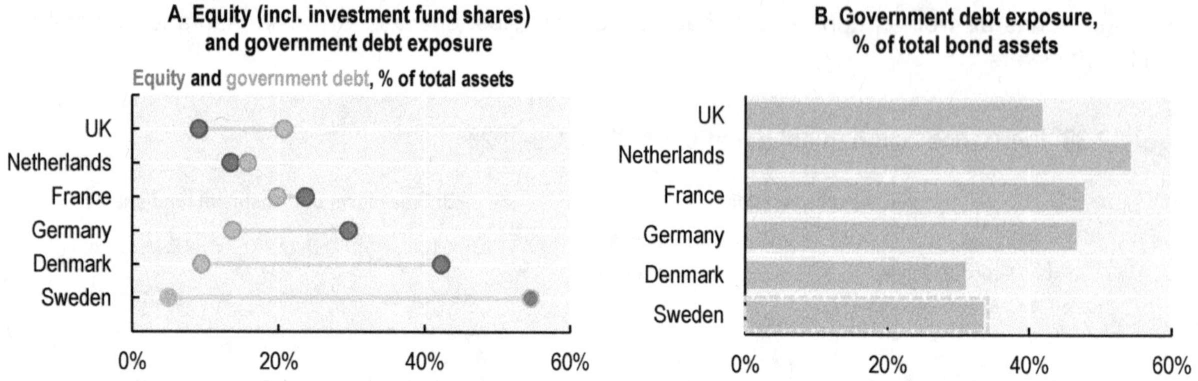

Note: In Panel B, total bond exposure excludes exposure through funds. It does not consider other debt instruments.
Source: OECD, EIOPA, Bank of England. Data covers insurance groups reporting under Solvency II.

The fact that Swedish insurance companies allocate a much larger share of their assets to equities than their peers on aggregate can partly be explained by the larger proportion of policyholder assets in unit- and index-linked portfolios (Figure 2.41, Panel A). In these insurance contracts, policyholders pay not just to cover the insurance premium, but an additional amount which is allocated to a diversified basket of assets, for which the policyholder assumes the investment risk. The asset allocation therefore tends to be less conservative than for other insurance contracts. This is not the only explanation, however, since Sweden exhibits the highest equity allocation among peer countries in both unit-linked and non-unit-linked portfolios (Panel B).

Figure 2.41. Insurance companies' asset allocation by portfolio type, Q3-2025

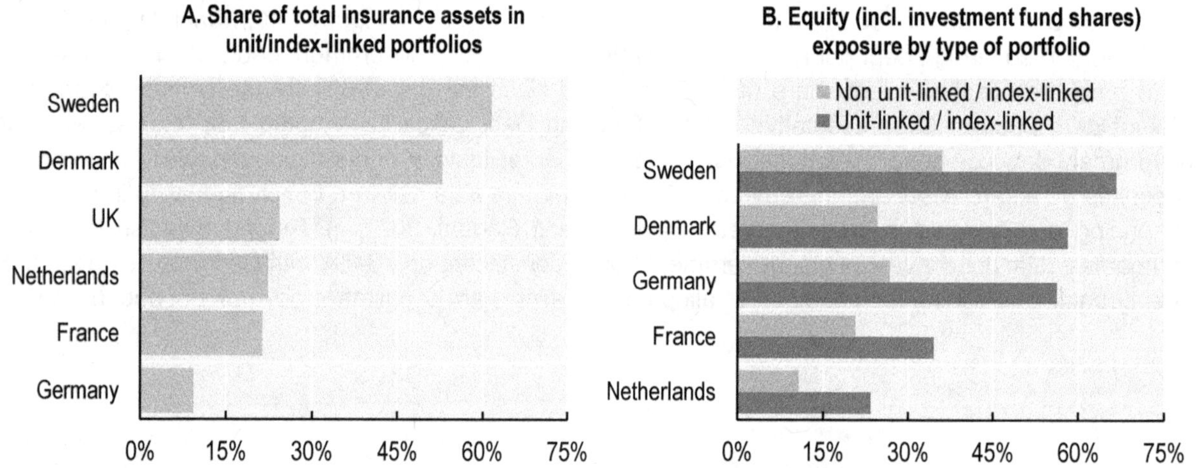

Note: Data covers insurance groups reporting under Solvency II. In Panel B, the breakdown by asset category and portfolio type is not available for the United Kingdom.
Source: EIOPA, Bank of England.

Box 2.7. Regulation of insurance companies

The Swedish insurance sector is regulated and supervised by the Swedish Financial Supervisory Authority (Finansinspektionen, FSA), a government agency under the Ministry of Finance. The primary legal frameworks to which these companies are subject include the Insurance Business Act (IBA), the Commission Delegated Regulation (EU) 2015/35 (Solvency II Regulation) – integrated into the IBA since its implementation in 2016 – and additional regulations and guidelines issued by the FSA and the European Insurance and Occupational Pensions Authority (EIOPA) (Vinge, 2022[62]). These regulations significantly influence which instruments insurance companies can invest in. Insurance undertakings are subject to strict capital requirements and investment restrictions. The Solvency Capital Requirement (SCR) under Solvency II mandates that insurers maintain sufficient capital to meet their obligations with 99.5% probability, and this cannot fall short of the Minimum Capital Requirement (MCR) which sets a threshold below which insurers cannot operate. Moreover, investment allocations must aim to limit risks and be made in instruments for which risks can be effectively identified, measured, and monitored. The use of derivatives is permitted only if they contribute to risk reduction or efficient portfolio management (Vinge, 2022[62]).

2.5.3. Investment funds

Investment funds have seen substantial growth in assets globally over recent decades and Sweden is no exception to this trend. Since the late 1970s, investment funds have served as an essential savings vehicle for Swedish households (see section 2.7). Their expansion has been further supported by increased investment from corporations and other institutions, making them an integral part of the country's financial system. The market value of funds domiciled in Sweden has increased 6.8 times in real terms since 2012, the year the ISK retail investment account was introduced (see Box 2.8). Direct equity investments followed a similar upward trend, reaching SEK 6.2 trillion (c. EUR 570 billion) at the end of 2025 (Figure 2.42).

Figure 2.42. Market value of Swedish investment funds

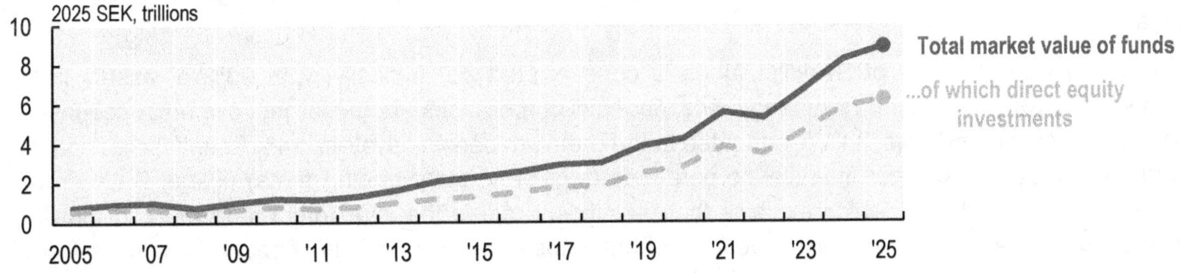

Note: Total market value of funds is adjusted to account for the value of debts and/or demands.
Source: Statistics Sweden (SCB).

Swedish-domiciled funds are heavily exposed to public equity markets, with 67% of their assets invested in listed shares (Figure 2.43, Panel A), nearly double peer countries' average allocation of 37%. Additionally, Swedish funds allocate 11% of their assets to other investment funds, which further boosts their overall exposure to equities. There have been notable changes in funds' asset composition over time. From 2005 to 2015, total equity market exposure decreased, but has since regained importance. This evolution has mainly been characterised by a rise in direct investments in foreign companies, which grew from 35% of funds' total market value in 2005 to 51% in 2025. In contrast, investments in domestic companies dropped from 33% to 18% over the same period. Additionally, Swedish funds have increased their investments in both domestic and foreign mutual funds (Panel B).

Figure 2.43. Investment funds' asset allocation

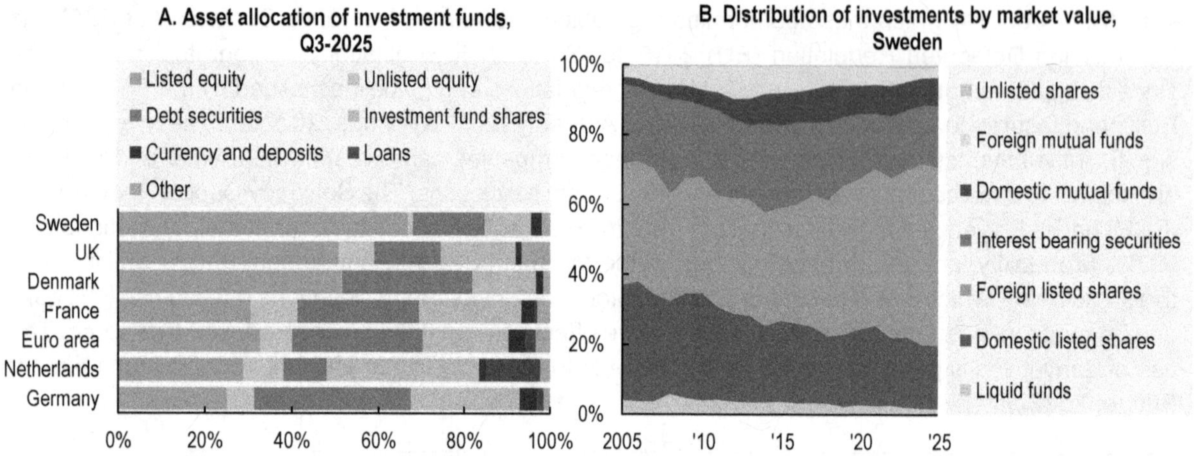

Note: Panel A refers to non-money market funds. The official UK statistics only disclose the split between listed and unlisted equity for domestic shares. The same split has been assumed to apply to foreign equities.
Source: ECB; Office for National Statistics (ONS); Statistics Sweden (SCB).

The strong preference for equity investments is also reflected in the distribution of funds based on their strategy. Equity funds are the largest category, accounting for 61% of the total value of funds (Figure 2.44, Panel A). Within this group, the share of assets in passive index funds has grown significantly over time, surpassing 20% in 2023 (Sveriges Riksbank, 2024[63]). This is in line with the growing global popularity of passive ETFs. In Europe, since the launch of the first ETF in 2000, the market has expanded significantly across asset classes, strategies and regions. By 2023, equity ETFs in Europe surpassed EUR 1 trillion in assets under management for the first time (LSEG, 2024[64]). Funds of funds (FoFs) rank second in terms of assets under management in Sweden. Unlike traditional funds, FoFs invest in other funds rather than individual securities. They can focus on, for example, mutual funds, hedge funds, private equity or real estate.

The ownership structure of Swedish funds is concentrated domestically, with 93% of assets held by domestic investors (Panel B.I). Among these, financial corporations are the largest owners, accounting for 77% of total assets. Of this, 33% is attributed to the premium pension system, 14% to unit-linked contracts, and the remainder to other financial corporations (e.g. proprietary trading firms) (Panel B.II). Premium pensions are mandatory, which explains their significant role in the investment fund market. Individuals can allocate their premiums to up to five investment funds from a wide range of options and have flexibility to adjust their allocations over time. If no choice is made, the premiums are automatically directed to the Seventh Swedish National Pension Fund, AP7 (see further discussion in section 2.5.1). Direct household holdings, separate from premium pensions and unit-linked insurance contracts, also represent a significant share (17%) of total ownership.

Figure 2.44. Composition and ownership of Swedish investment funds by market value, end-2025

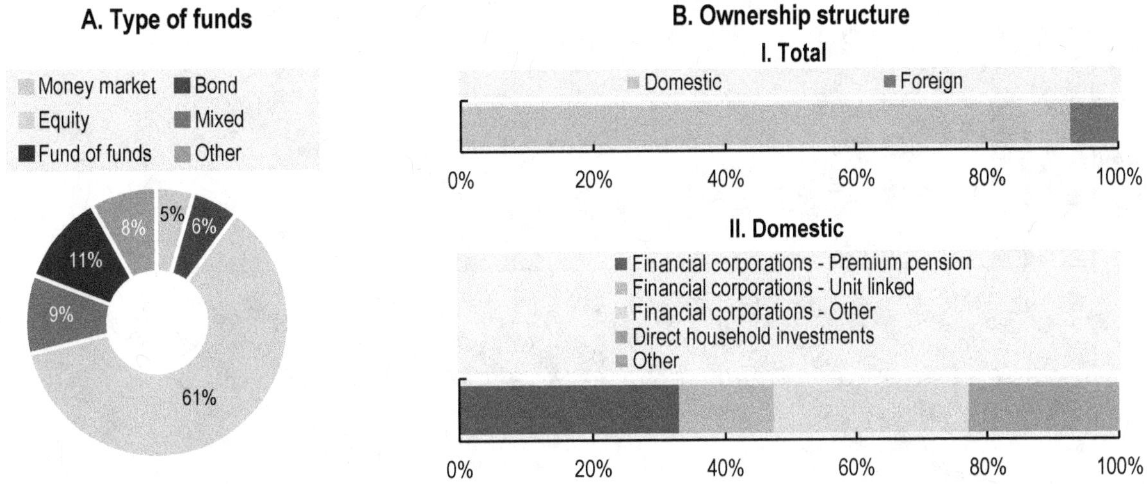

Note: In Panel B the "other" category includes non-financial corporations, local government, social security funds, non-profit institutions serving households and other domestic owners.
Source: Statistics Sweden (SCB).

2.6. Investment companies/family owners

Family-owned investment companies have contributed to Sweden's economic development and corporate landscape since its industrialisation in the late 19th and early 20th centuries. Through their investment firms, families such as the Wallenbergs, the Lundbergs, and the Stenbecks have maintained significant ownership stakes in flagship companies for decades. The Wallenberg family, for instance, controls Investor AB, one of the largest investment companies in Europe, which alone owns over 4% of total Swedish public equity market capitalisation (Figure 2.45). Similarly, Industrivärden AB, LE Lundbergföretagen, Melker Schörling and Investment AB Latour, all controlled by their founding families, also rank among the largest owners of Swedish public equity. Together, these five family-owned investment firms own more than 8% of all Swedish public equity market capitalisation.

This ownership model has been supported by dual class share structures, which allow for a higher proportion of voting rights than capital stakes. As a result, these families have been able to take an active role in shaping Swedish corporate governance from an early stage. Since the 1930s, they have also themselves relied on public markets to raise capital, developing in parallel with the Swedish equity markets, which has served to align their interests with broad market growth and development.

Figure 2.45. Largest owners of publicly listed equities in Sweden

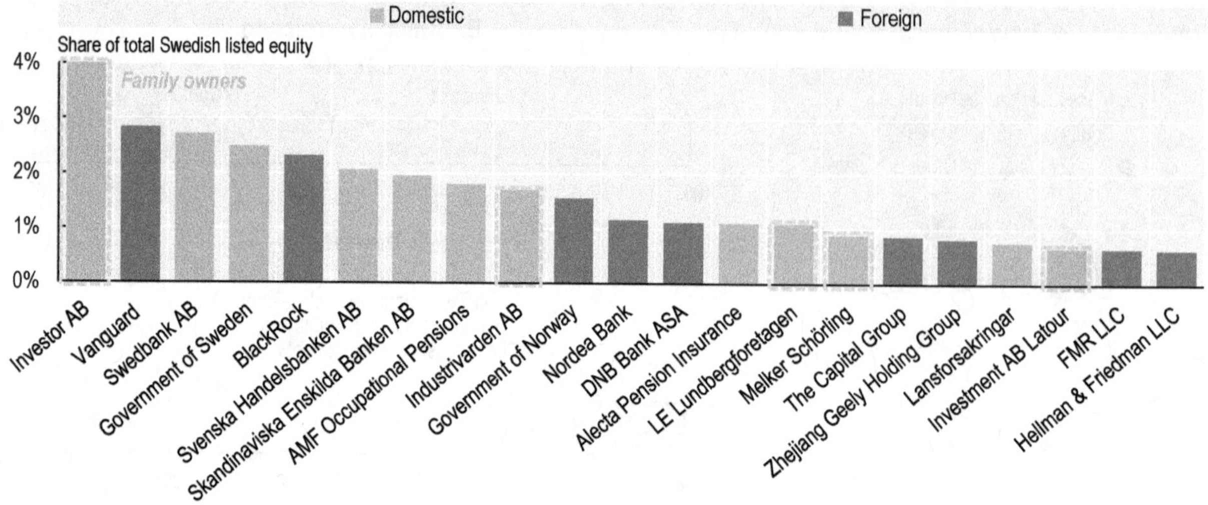

Note: The figure shows ultimate parent names, so banks here refer to the funds operated by these banks.
Source: OECD Capital Market Series dataset, FactSet, LSEG and Bloomberg, see Annex for details.

The major family-owned investment firms in Sweden typically have long-term investment horizons. According to some market participants, this is a factor that helps them build deep expertise about their portfolio companies and institutional knowledge of market dynamics, enabling a more active and long-term ownership role. For instance, through Investor AB, the Wallenberg family owns major stakes in blue-chip companies like ABB, Atlas Copco and SEB. Similarly, the Lundberg, Douglas and Schörling families hold substantial stakes in well-known companies such as Volvo, Sandvik and Assa Alboy through their investment companies (Table 2.2).

Table 2.2. Family ownership of Swedish equities through investment companies

Investment company name	Equity held as % of total Swedish market cap.	Year of establishment	Holding family	Top 3 investee companies by market cap.
Investor AB	4%	1916	Wallenberg family	ABB Atlas Copco AstraZeneca
Industrivärden	1.7%	1944	Lundberg family	Sandvik Volvo Svenska Hadelsbanken
LE Lundbergföretagen	1.1%	1944	Lundberg family	Industrivärden Indutrade Holmen
Melker Schörling	1%	1998	Schörling family	AAK Assa Abloy Hexagon
Investment AB Latour	0.7%	1985	Douglas family	Assa Abloy Sweco Tomra Systems
Lannebo Kapitalforvaltning AB	0.6%	1947	Dinkelspiel family	Nordnet Microsoft NVIDIA

Note: Excludes individual investors.
Source: (Lundbergs[65]), https://www.lundbergforetagen.se/en/equity-holdings, (Schorling[66]), https://www.schorlingab.se/en/our-holdings#assa-abloy, OECD Capital Market Series dataset, FactSet, LSEG and Bloomberg, see Annex for details.

2.7. Households as investors

Retail investment plays a fundamental role in capital market development, channelling household savings into the real economy and thereby increasing the funds available to finance productive investment. Equally importantly, it also directly benefits households, offering them opportunities to partake in corporate wealth creation and enhance financial well-being. Additionally, it can contribute to better local market functioning, notably increased liquidity, in particular for smaller company stocks.

Household involvement in capital markets (including indirect investments through investment funds, insurance, and pension funds) is substantially higher in Sweden than in the EU overall. This is driven by several factors, such as higher income and savings levels, the availability and simplicity of savings vehicles that meet consumer needs, as well as relatively high levels of financial literacy.

Sweden's GDP per capita, measured in USD PPPs, has consistently remained higher than that of the EU and, until 2021, also marginally above the average of peer countries (i.e. Denmark, France, Germany, the Netherlands and the UK) (Figure 2.46, Panel A). As economic output rises, household income tends to increase, enabling them to allocate a smaller portion to essential expenses and direct more of their earnings towards savings, which in turn influences investment in capital markets. Extensive public social safety nets also mean that households do not need to allocate substantial portions of private savings to, for example, health insurance, leaving more funds available for investment (although to the extent that these services are funded by higher taxes, it also serves to reduce the disposable income available for saving, all else being equal). This is reflected in Sweden's savings rate, which has persistently been one of the highest among its peers. The savings rate saw a substantial increase in 2020 following the COVID-19 pandemic, although gradually approached pre-pandemic levels in the following years. A similar trend is also observed in other countries (Panel B).

Figure 2.46. GDP per capita and savings rate

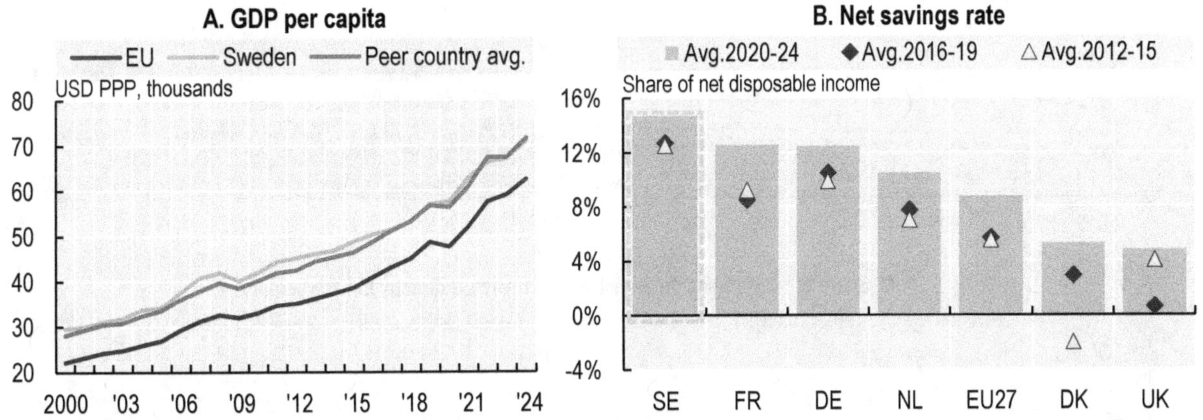

Note: In Panel A, GDP per capital is expressed in current international dollars, converted by a purchasing power parity (PPP) conversion factor. In Panel B, the household savings rate is defined as the share of household net disposable income that is saved. See endnotes for commentary on data changes in this figure.
Source: OECD, World Bank.

Swedish households' high savings are also reflected in their financial assets, which significantly exceed both the EU aggregate and the peer country average, with the gap widening over time (Figure 2.47, Panel A). However, greater growth in financial wealth in Sweden compared to peer countries is not just a matter of a higher savings rate. It is also related to the propensity to save through capital markets. As of the third quarter of 2025, Swedish households allocated the smallest share of their financial assets to currency and deposits among peers, at 12%. In contrast, they ranked first, together with Germany, in the share allocated to listed equities (7.1%) and second in investment fund shares (10%) (Panel B).

According to Nasdaq figures, Sweden has the highest level of retail investor activity among the Nordic countries. In July 2022, retail investors represented 12% of total turnover on Sweden's main market. Retail activity is especially important for smaller companies: in the first seven months of 2022, retail clients accounted for nearly 30% of total trading volume on the First North Growth Market. Additionally, they play a key role in providing liquidity to new equity issuances. For example, in 2021, a year of substantial IPO activity (see section 2.1), retail investors accounted for 35% of the trading in the 10 days following Volvo Car's IPO (one of Sweden's largest ever public offerings). Retail participation was even higher for the IPO of CTEK, reaching 45% (Nasdaq, 2022[67]). Over the last decade, the share of financial assets invested directly in listed equity has consistently been higher in Sweden than in peer countries and has trended upward, reaching a peak of 9% in 2021 (Panel C).

Consultations with market participants indicate that a high level of retail investment has contributed to the success of the self-regulatory model discussed in Box 2.1, by creating a significant reputation risk tied to any potential failure of the capital market system as a whole. Extensive household participation in these markets makes the preservation of investor trust essential to maintaining public legitimacy, and market stakeholders therefore have strong incentives to correct and avoid shortcomings that could damage their credibility.

Figure 2.47. Households' financial assets

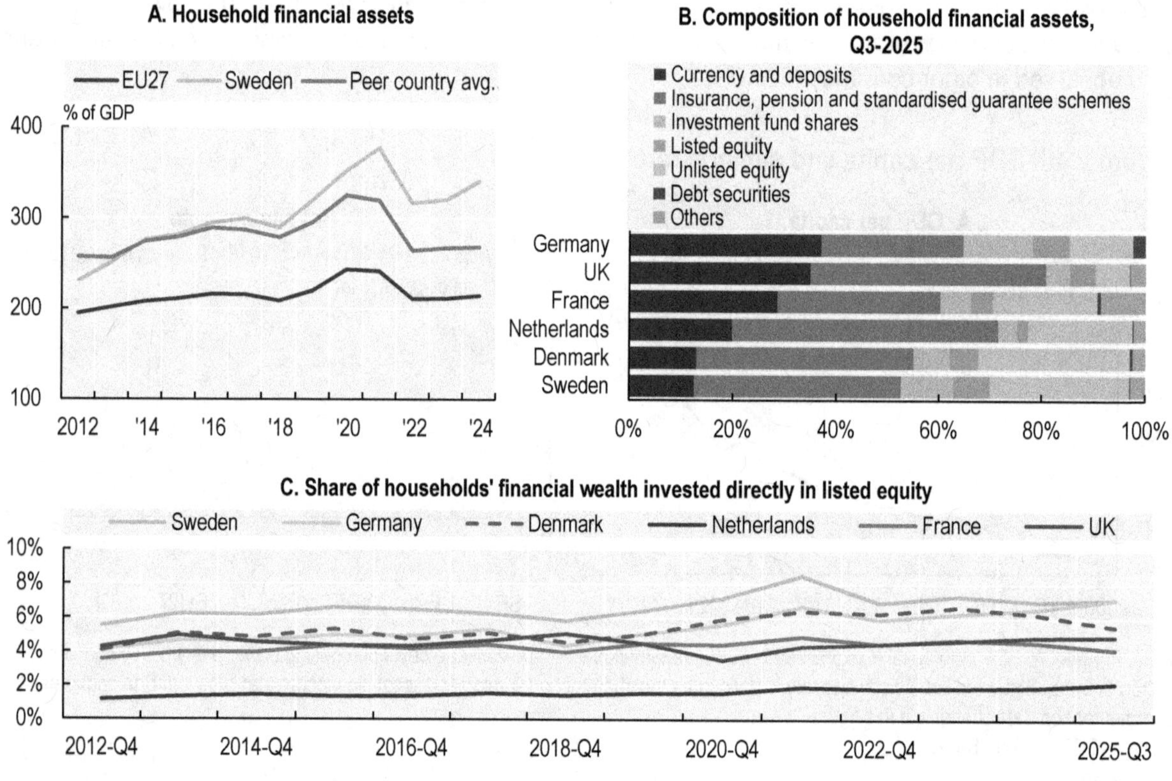

Note: In Panel A, UK values between 2020 and 2023 are based on OECD calculations. EU-level data only available until 2022. The peer countries included in the average are Denmark, France, Germany, the Netherlands and the United Kingdom. The official UK statistics used in Panel B only disclose the split between listed and unlisted equity for domestic shares. The same split has been assumed to apply to foreign equities. Includes the premium component of the Swedish public pension system.
Source: Eurostat; ECB; Office for National Statistics (ONS).

Despite significant household assets held in equities, the share of the population with direct holdings of shares in companies listed on Swedish markets has declined steadily over time, falling from 22% in 2000 to 9% in 2025 (Figure 2.48, Panel A). This downward trend is evident across all age groups, with the most pronounced absolute decline taking place among 55 to 64-year-olds, for whom participation dropped by more than 20 percentage points (from 36.3% in 2000 to 14.4% in 2025). The largest relative decline occurred among the population aged under 18 and 18 to 24-year olds, whose direct participation in equity markets decreased by 92%, from 7.5% to 0.6% and 70%, from 14.7% to 4.4%, respectively, during the same period (Panel B).

Figure 2.48. Share of the population with direct ownership stakes in companies listed on Swedish equity markets

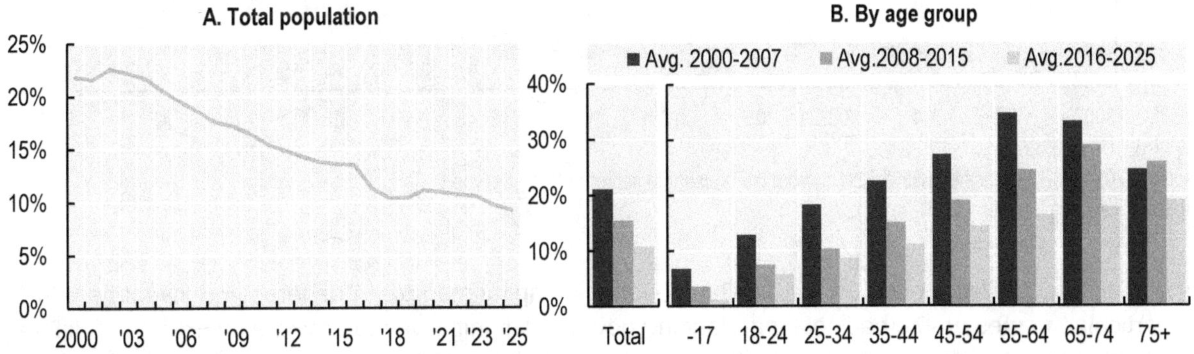

Note: Includes unlisted classes of stock in quoted companies.
Source: Statistics Sweden (SCB).

There has been a corresponding, albeit lesser, decrease in the share of total market value of companies listed on Swedish equity markets held directly by households (Figure 2.49). This share has remained around 12% since 2015, suggesting a growing concentration of direct holdings among fewer individuals. In other words, although fewer people participate directly in equity markets, those who do tend to hold greater amounts.

Figure 2.49. Share of household ownership in companies listed on Swedish public equity markets

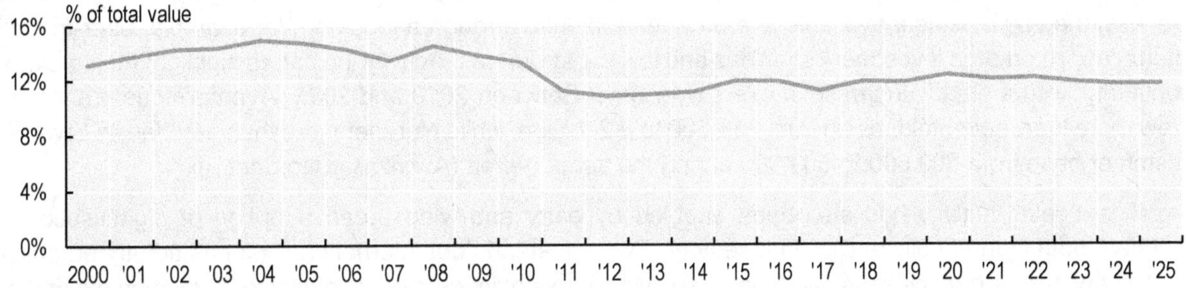

Source: Statistics Sweden (SCB).

However, the decrease in direct retail participation does not necessarily imply a reduction in household capital market participation. It could equally be a reflection of the growing prominence and popularity of other investment products, notably passive index funds. Indeed, in parallel to the decrease in direct retail participation, there has been a sharp increase in indirect equity holdings through investment funds, indicating a shift in preference as more affordable investment options have emerged in recent years. The rise has been particularly notable for equity and mixed funds, as well as for funds-of-funds (Figure 2.50).

Figure 2.50. Households' direct investments in funds

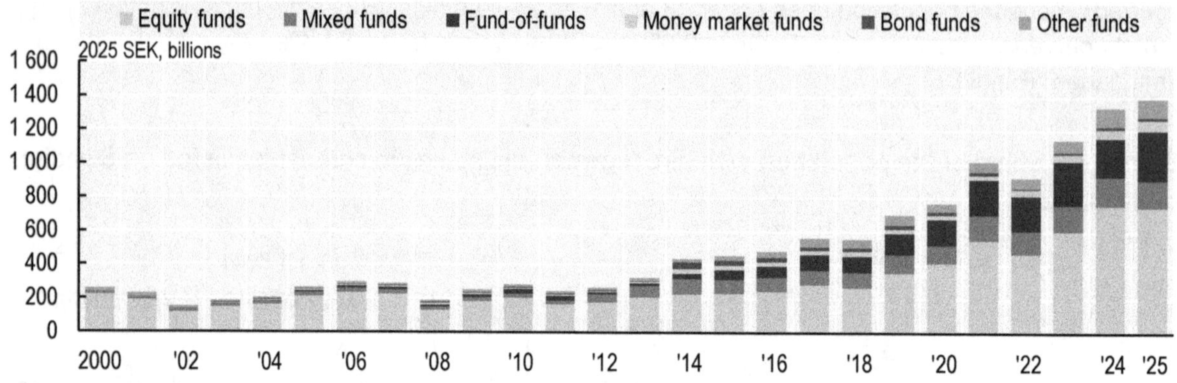

Note: In 2014 SCB reclassified SEK 16 billion from the household sector to foreign owners.
Source: Statistics Sweden (SCB).

The widespread participation of Swedish households in capital markets in general, and investment funds in particular, comes on the back of long-standing government initiatives to promote ownership of different financial assets. Funds in which contributions were partially deductible against income tax were introduced already in the late 1970s to encourage household savings. Following this development, the *Allemansspar* savings programme was launched in 1984, enabling savers to put their money in an account or invest in different types of funds (*Allemansfonder*) with tax-free returns. These products became very popular, which persisted even after the removal of tax benefits in 1997 (Fondbolagens förening[68]). The introduction of the premium pension system in 1994 served to further strengthen household interest in capital markets (see section 2.5.1). More recently, in 2012, the government introduced a dedicated Investment Savings Accounts (ISK) with simplified taxation. Instead of taxing capital gains at the point of sale, a flat rate is applied to the total value of the account each year (Box 2.8). ISKs have become extremely popular, further incentivising savings in capital markets, notably funds and equities.

Since the early 2000s, digital investment platforms such as Avanza and Nordnet have also played a significant role in expanding Swedish retail engagement in capital markets by simplifying the investment process, thereby making it available to a broader audience through a focus on, for example, user-friendly interfaces, automated investment solutions and low fee structures. Activity indicators highlight their growing popularity, with a steady increase in users over time. Between 2013 and 2025, Avanza's customer base grew more than sevenfold, rising from 316 500 to 2.2 million, while Nordnet more than doubled its Swedish customer base from 209 600 to 509 900 during the same period (Avanza[69]; Nordnet[18]).

Significant retail activity has also been enabled by early and widespread adoption of digitalisation in Sweden, both in the public and private sectors. Sweden stands out internationally for its advanced online public services for both citizens and businesses with levels of investment in digital technologies exceeding the EU average (EC, 2023[70]). This commitment to digitalisation helps simplify activities like investment and enhances access to online services. A notable example is the electronic identification tool BankID, used to access public and banking services as well as to sign documents electronically. The country's corporate sector also tends to exhibit a strong uptake of technology-driven solutions (EC, 2024[71]).

Another factor positively influencing participation in equity markets is a high degree of financial literacy. Recognising this, the European Commission included it as part of its Capital Markets Union action plan (EC[72]). Additionally, developing a financial literacy strategy is a key measure of the Savings and

Investments Union (EC, 2025[73]). Sweden ranks ninth out of 39 countries in the latest OECD/INFE international survey of adult financial literacy, reflecting its strong overall literacy levels while also highlighting areas for potential improvement. Swedish individuals stand out in particular when it comes to financial attitudes (i.e. beliefs and values related to money management), where they rank 3rd (Figure 2.51).

Box 2.8. The Swedish Investment Savings Account (ISK)

The Swedish Investment Savings Account (*investeringssparkonto*, ISK) is a flat-taxed investment account introduced by the Swedish government in 2012, designed to simplify the management of financial securities such as shares by retail investors. The account is available to people of all ages, making it a viable option for children as well. Ownership is individual.

Unlike traditional trading accounts, ISK accounts do not require individuals to report or pay capital gains taxes upon disposal. Instead, account holders are subject to a standardised annual tax, which is applied to the total market value of the assets held in the account (calculated as the sum of the market value of all assets at the beginning of each quarter, plus the sum of all deposits into the account, divided by four). This value is then multiplied by the government borrowing rate in the previous year plus one percentage point, with a minimum rate of 1.25%, to obtain a notional capital income. The resulting amount is then taxed at a flat rate of 30%, regardless of whether there have been actual capital gains or losses (or indeed any disposals at all) within the fiscal year. Importantly, taxpayers themselves are not responsible for these calculations; they are done by the institution managing the ISK account (e.g. a bank or fund management company), which then reports the notional capital income to the Swedish tax authority.

This simplified taxation model has contributed to the strong popularity of ISK accounts since their introduction in 2012, reaching approximately 3.8 million users (well over a third of the total population) in 2023 (Fondbolagens förening, 2024[74]). Despite their widespread adoption, the tax advantages that have typically been assumed to be associated with ISK accounts are not unambiguous. For one, any tax benefits assume excess returns above the standard tax rate (which was often at the lower bound in recent years, but which has increased sharply following increases in policy rates and government borrowing costs since 2022). In a 2018 analysis, the Swedish National Audit Office also noted that ISK accounts may not offer clear tax benefits, especially for very long holding periods (NAO, 2018[75]). In 2024 the government proposed changes to introduce unequivocal fiscal benefits to ISK accounts. Starting in 2025, the first SEK 150 000 (c. EUR 13 000) saved in an ISK or endowment insurance account was tax-exempt, a threshold that increased to SEK 300 000 (c. EUR 27 500) in 2026.

Figure 2.51. Levels of adult financial literacy

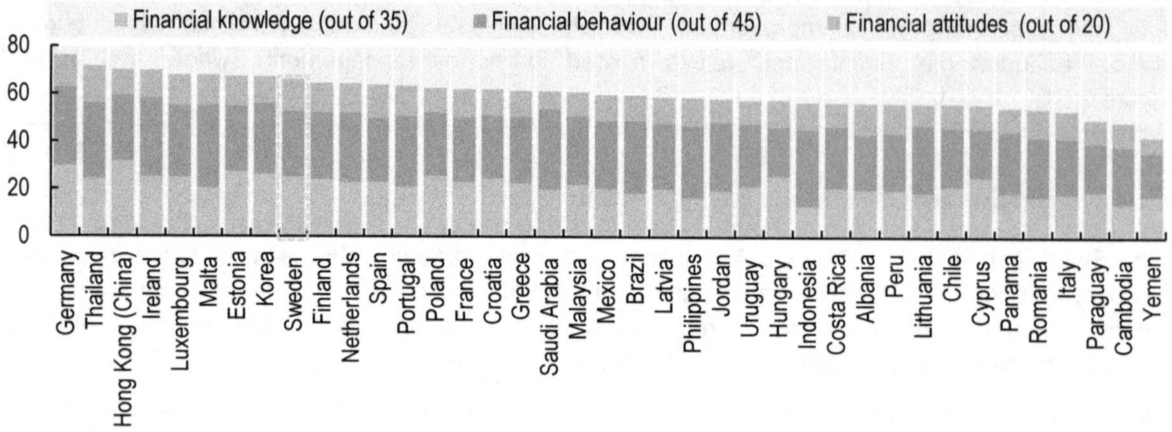

Source: OECD/INFE (2023[76]), OECD/INFE 2023 International Survey of Adult Financial Literacy, https://read.oecd.org/10.1787/56003a32-en.

Over the past decades, several initiatives have been launched to improve financial literacy in Sweden, targeting key demographics. In 2010, the Swedish National Network on Financial Education was established, bringing together authorities, organisations and companies to enhance citizens' understanding of personal finance through educational projects (The Swedish National Network on Financial Education[77]). The initiatives include courses for professionals who support people in financial vulnerability, pensioners, and students in colleges and universities. Moreover, *Unga Aktiesparare* (Young Stock Savers) is a non-profit association founded in 1990, dedicated to helping young people build financial literacy and investment skills. Through its numerous local branches across the country, the organisation offers educational programmes, networking events, and other activities. *Unga Aktiesparare* also runs the "Young Private Finances" project, which reaches around 30 000 high school students each year, providing personal financial education through nationwide school visits (Unga Aktiesparare[78]). Sweden has also integrated financial education into the school curriculum and participates in Global Money Week, a campaign organised by the OECD that aims to raise awareness about the importance of financial literacy from an early age.

References

Act (2000:192) (2000), *Act (2000:192) on public pension funds (AP funds)*, Ministry of Finance FMA FPM, https://www.riksdagen.se/sv/dokument-och-lagar/dokument/svensk-forfattningssamling/lag-2000192-om-allmanna-pensionsfonder_sfs-2000-192/#K1. [53]

AP2 (n.d.), *AP6 has concluded its operations*, https://ap2.se/en/about-ap2/about-ap6/. [48]

AP2 (n.d.), *Historik*, https://ap2.se/om/vart-uppdrag/ett-unikt-pensionssystem/historik/. [41]

AP2 (n.d.), *Our mission*, https://ap2.se/en/about-ap2/our-mission/. [44]

AP4 (n.d.), *Första AP-fonden (AP1) har avvecklats*, https://www.ap4.se/om-ap4/om-ap1/. [47]

AP6 (2024), *Consolidation during a challenging year*, https://www.ap6.se/en/consolidation-during-a-challenging-year/. [55]

AP7 (n.d.), *AP7 - About us - Our approach*, https://www.ap7.se/english/about-us/our-approach/. [52]

Avanza (n.d.), *Annual and interim reports*, https://investors.avanza.se/en/ir/reports/annual-and-interim-reports/. [69]

Babalos, V. and S. Stavroyiannis (2020), "Pension funds and stock market development in OECD countries: Novel evidence from a panel VAR☆", *Finance Research Letters*, Vol. 34, https://doi.org/10.1016/j.frl.2019.07.020. [35]

Bain & Company (2024), *Global Private Equity Report 2024*, https://www.bain.com/globalassets/noindex/2024/bain_report_global-private-equity-report-2024.pdf. [23]

Bjellerup, M. and J. Rådahl (2023), *Long-term conditions for debt management*, https://www.riksgalden.se/contentassets/ea257dc12453430186b47e2bcfe20376/debt-office-commentary-long-term-conditions-for-debt-management.pdf. [61]

Collectum (n.d.), *Retirement pension*, https://collectum.se/en/startpage/companies/itp-itpk-and-tgl/retirement-pension. [57]

Confederation of Swedish Enterprise (2023), *Dual class share structures with differentiated voting rights: a Swedish perspective*, https://www.svensktnaringsliv.se/bilder_och_dokument/evagop_final-february-2023-dual-class-share-structurespdf_1195673.html/FINAL+February+2023+Dual+class+share+structures_1.pdf. [30]

EC (2025), *The Savings and Investments Union - Connecting savings and productive investments*, https://finance.ec.europa.eu/document/download/2701e5bb-e5e8-484e-b206-6bb5e6a27044_en?filename=250319-factsheet-siu_en.pdf. [73]

EC (2024), *Report on the state of the Digital Decade 2024 - 30- Annex 3 Sweden Executive summary*, https://digital-strategy.ec.europa.eu/en/library/report-state-digital-decade-2024. [71]

EC (2023), *Digital Decade report 2023 - Sweden*, https://digital-strategy.ec.europa.eu/en/library/country-reports-digital-decade-report-2023. [70]

EC (n.d.), *Action 7 - Empowering citizens through financial literacy*, https://finance.ec.europa.eu/capital-markets-union-and-financial-markets/capital-markets-union/capital-markets-union-2020-action-plan/action-7-empowering-citizens-through-financial-literacy_en. [72]

Edebalk, P. (2013), "1913 års pensionsförsäkring – den första allmänna socialförsäkringen", *Socialvetenskaplig tidskrift*, Vol. 3-4, pp. 241-249, https://socvet.se/article/view/2435. [39]

EQT (n.d.), *About*, https://eqtgroup.com/about/history/. [22]

ESMA (2023), *National thresholds below which the obligation to publish a prospectus does not apply*, https://www.esma.europa.eu/sites/default/files/library/esma31-62-1193_prospectus_thresholds.pdf. [3]

European Commission (2025), *European Innovation Scoreboard*, https://research-and-innovation.ec.europa.eu/statistics/performance-indicators/european-innovation-scoreboard_en#eis-interactive-tool. [14]

European Commission (2022), *Directive of the European Parliment and of the Council on multiple-vote share structures in companies that seek the admission to trading of their shares on an SME growth market*, https://eur-lex.europa.eu/legal-content/EN/TXT/?uri=CELEX:52022PC0761. [32]

EY (2025), *Transaction Trends - Swedish M&A update – Q4 2024*, https://mb.cision.com/Main/1179/4094393/3216729.pdf. [13]

Finansinspektionen (2016), *Guidance and Instructions - Listed and MTF companies*, https://www.fi.se/contentassets/395fd56d8ecc4dda968f17e073f572a6/vaglednbors_mtf_7okt2016_eng.pdf. [15]

Flicker, M. (2004), "Securities Trading on the Internet", *The Internet Encyclopedia*, https://doi.org/10.1002/047148296X.tie159. [12]

Fondbolagens förening (2024), *The investment savings account in focus*, https://www.fondbolagen.se/globalassets/faktaindex/studier-o-undersokningar/isk/isk-rapport-okt-2024_eng.pdf. [74]

Fondbolagens förening (n.d.), *How Sweden became a world leader in fund saving*, https://www.fondbolagen.se/en/Facts_Indices/sweden-a-world-champion-in-fund-savings/. [68]

Gilson, R. (2014), *The Nordic Model of Corporate Governance: The Role of Ownership*, SNS Publishing, https://scholarship.law.columbia.edu/faculty_scholarship/1895/. [34]

Hagströmer, B. (2022), "Market Fragmentation in Europe", *SSRN Electronic Journal*, https://doi.org/10.2139/SSRN.4274523. [10]

Hanselaar, R., R. Stulz and M. van Dijk (2019), "Do firms issue more equity when markets become more liquid?", *Journal of Financial Economics*, Vol. 133/1, pp. 64-82, https://doi.org/10.1016/J.JFINECO.2018.12.004. [8]

Investment & Pensions Europe (2023), *Sweden should probe ditching AP funds' mandatory forex hedging, says report*, https://www.ipe.com/news/sweden-should-probe-ditching-ap-funds-mandatory-forex-hedging-says-report/10065787.article. [54]

ISS (2023), *Dual Class Share Structures: The European Experience*, https://insights.issgovernance.com/posts/dual-class-share-structures-the-european-experience/ (accessed on 22 November 2024). [29]

Kastiel, K. and Y. Nili (2024), "The Rise of Private Equity Continuation Funds", *University of Pennsylvania Law Review*, Vol. 172, pp. 1601-1666, https://scholarship.law.upenn.edu/cgi/viewcontent.cgi?article=9858&context=penn_law_review. [24]

Konsumenternas (n.d.), *Tjänstepension*, https://www.konsumenternas.se/sparande--pension/pension/tjanstepension/kollektivavtalade-tjanstepensioner/. [58]

Lekvall, P. (2014), *(ed.) The Nordic Corporate Governance Model*, SNS Publishing, https://snsse.cdn.triggerfish.cloud/uploads/2020/02/the_nordic_corporate_governance_model_1.pdf. [33]

LSEG (2024), *Happy Birthday ETF Industry—A Brief History of the European ETF Industry*, https://lipperalpha.refinitiv.com/reports/2024/04/happy-birthday-etf-industry-a-brief-history-of-the-european-etf-industry-2/. [64]

Lundbergs (n.d.), *Equity holdings*, https://www.lundbergforetagen.se/en/equity-holdings (accessed on 2 April 2026). [65]

Medina, A., A. de la Cruz and Y. Tang (2022), "Corporate ownership and concentration", *OECD Corporate Governance Working Papers*, No. 27, OECD Publishing, Paris, https://doi.org/10.1787/bc3adca3-en. [2]

NAO (2018), *Investment savings account - a simple form of saving in a complex tax system*, https://www.riksrevisionen.se/download/18.59eb8325166dd783b805f2d8/1541659916695/RiR_2018_19_ENGLISH.pdf. [75]

Nasdaq (2026), *Certified Advisers as of February 17, 2026*, https://www.nasdaq.com/docs/2026/02/18/certified-advisers-2026-week-8.pdf. [17]

Nasdaq (2023), *Nasdaq Celebrates 130 Switches From Nasdaq First North Growth Market to Nordic Main Markets*, https://www.nasdaq.com/articles/130th-switch-to-main-markets. [1]

Nasdaq (2023), *Nasdaq introduces an auction Nasdaq introduces an auction shares on Nasdaq First North Growth Market*, https://www.nasdaq.com/press-release/nasdaq-introduces-an-auction-model-to-support-less-liquid-shares-on-nasdaq-first. [9]

Nasdaq (2022), *4 takeaways from recent retail activity in Nordic & Baltic markets*, https://www.nasdaq.com/docs/2022/09/27/4-Key-Takeaways-from-Recent-Retail-Activity-in-Nordics-and-Baltics-Report.pdf. [67]

Nasdaq (2015), *Guide to becoming a Certified Adviser on First North*, https://www.nasdaq.com/docs/first-north-ca-guide.pdf. [16]

Nasdaq (n.d.), *Listing Guide to Nasdaq First North Growth Market*, https://www.nasdaq.com/docs/Going_Public_Listing_guide_to_Nasdaq_First_North_GM.pdf. [5]

Nenova, T. (2003), "The Value of Corporate Voting Rights and Control: A Crosscountry Analysis", *The Journal of Financial Economic 68*, https://doi.org/10.1016/s0304-405x(03)00069-2. [4]

Niggemann, T. and J. Rocholl (2010), "Pension Funding and Capital Market Development", *SSRN*, https://doi.org/10.2139/ssrn.1571126. [36]

Nordic Growth Market (2024), *Rules - Nordic SME*, https://www.ngm.se/hubfs/Rules%20-%20Nordic%20SME_mark-up-1.pdf. [6]

Nordnet (n.d.), *Reports*, https://nordnetab.com/investors/financials/. [18]

OECD (2025), *Pensions at a Glance 2025: OECD and G20 Indicators*, OECD Publishing, https://www.oecd.org/en/publications/pensions-at-a-glance-2025_e40274c1-en.html. [56]

OECD (2025), *Venture capital investments (market statistics)*, http://data-explorer.oecd.org/s/1o9. [27]

OECD (2023), "OECD/INFE 2023 International Survey of Adult Financial Literacy", *OECD Business and Finance Policy Papers*, No. 39, OECD Publishing, Paris, https://doi.org/10.1787/56003a32-en. [76]

OECD (2016), "Changing business models of stock exchanges and stock market fragmentation", in *OECD Business and Finance Outlook 2016*, OECD Publishing, Paris, https://doi.org/10.1787/9789264257573-9-en. [11]

Pereira, J. (2023), "Once Bitten, Twice Shy - Multiple Voting Shares in Continental Europe", *The Journal of International Business & Law*, Vol. 22/2, https://www.hofstrajibl.org/wp-content/uploads/2023/07/Periera-Step-2-complete-PDF.pdf. [31]

PitchBook (2026), *Nordic Private Capital Breakdown*, https://pitchbook.brightspotcdn.com/81/62/bdb2ffcd4add9d798a4b6509122a/2026-nordic-private-capital-breakdown.pdf. [25]

PitchBook (2024), *2024 Nordic Private Capital Breakdown*, https://files.pitchbook.com/website/files/pdf/2024_Nordic_Private_Capital_Breakdown.pdf. [26]

PitchBook (2023), *2022 Annual European PE Breakdown*, https://files.pitchbook.com/website/files/pdf/2022_Annual_European_PE_Breakdown.pdf. [20]

Private Equity International (2025), *PEI 300: The world's largest private equity firms*, https://www.privateequityinternational.com/pei-300/#pei-300-full-ranking. [21]

Regeringskansliet (2020), *The Swedish pension system and pension projections until 2070*, https://economy-finance.ec.europa.eu/system/files/2021-05/se_-_ar_2021_final_pension_fiche.pdf. [42]

Riksbanken (2024), *Private equity: a growing market in transition*, https://www.riksbank.se/globalassets/media/rapporter/fsr/fordjupningar/svenska/2024/240529/private-equity-en-vaxande-marknad-i-forandring-fordjupning-i-finansiell-stabilitetsrapport-2024_1.pdf. [19]

Riksgälden (2024), *Swedish central government debt continued to decrease in 2023*, https://www.riksgalden.se/fi/press-and-publications/press-releases-and-news/news/2024/swedish-central-government-debt-continued-to-decrease-in-2023/. [60]

Schorling (n.d.), *Our holdings*, https://www.schorlingab.se/en/our-holdings#assa-abloy (accessed on 2 April 2026). [66]

Spotlight Stock Market (2023), *Spotlight's regulations*, https://ir.spotlightstockmarket.com/media/5frictxi/spotlights-regulations-2023-12-01.pdf. [7]

Svensk Försäkring (2025), *Insurance in Sweden 2015-2024*, https://www.svenskforsakring.se/globalassets/publikationer/forsakringar-i-sverige/insurance-in-sweden-2015-2024.pdf/. [59]

Sveriges Riksbank (2024), *The Swedish Financial Market 2024*, https://www.riksbank.se/globalassets/media/rapporter/den-svenska-finansmarknaden/engelska/2024/the-swedish-financial-market-2024.pdf. [63]

Swedish Parliament (2025), *Ja till färre AP-fonder och skärpta kompetenskrav på styrelser*, https://www.riksdagen.se/sv/aktuellt/aktuelltnotiser/2025/maj/15/ja-till-farre-ap-fonder-och-skarpta-kompetenskrav_cms55505564-1f8c-4da7-8a84-670750d99f68sv/. [46]

Swedish Parliament (2020), *Redovisning av AP-fondernas verksamhet t.o.m. 2019*, https://www.riksdagen.se/sv/dokument-och-lagar/dokument/skrivelse/redovisning-av-ap-fondernas-verksamhet-t.o.m.-2019_h703130/html/. [45]

Swedish Pension Agency (2024), *Statistik om premiepensionen*, https://www.pensionsmyndigheten.se/statistik-och-rapporter/statistik/statistik-for-premiepension. [51]

Swedish Pension Agency (n.d.), *Ansök om allmän pension - frågor och svar*, https://www.pensionsmyndigheten.se/vanliga-fragor-och-svar-om-pension/vanliga-fragor/fragor-och-svar-om-att-ansoka-om-pension. [50]

Swedish Pension Agency (n.d.), *Det gamla ATP-systemet*, https://www.pensionsmyndigheten.se/forsta-din-pension/om-pensionssystemet/det-gamla-atp-systemet. [40]

Swedish Pension Agency (n.d.), *Fonder - premiepensionsfonder och fondbyte - frågor och svar*, https://www.pensionsmyndigheten.se/vanliga-fragor-och-svar-om-pension/vanliga-fragor/fragor-och-svar-om-premiepensionsfonder-och-fondbyte. [49]

Swedish Pension Agency (n.d.), *National public pension*, https://www.pensionsmyndigheten.se/other-languages/english-engelska/english-engelska/national-public-pension. [43]

Swedish Pensions Agency (2026), *Official Statistics of Sweden*, https://www.pensionsmyndigheten.se/statistik-och-rapporter/statistik/sveriges-officiella-statistik. [38]

Swedish Securities Market Association (2024), *The Swedish securities market*, https://svenskvardepappersmarknad.se/en/verksamheten/vardepappersmarknaden/ (accessed on 7 April 2026). [28]

The Swedish National Network on Financial Education (n.d.), *The Swedish National Network on Financial Education*, https://gilladinekonomi.se/english/. [77]

Unga Aktiesparare (n.d.), *About us*, https://www.ungaaktiesparare.se/om-oss/. [78]

US Federal Reserve (2026), *Z.1 Financial Accounts of the United States, Table L.117 Private and Public Pension Funds*, https://www.federalreserve.gov/releases/z1/20260319/z1.pdf. [37]

Vinge (2022), *Insurance services in Sweden*, https://www.vinge.se/media/eohd0fvd/insurance-services-in-sweden-2022-final.pdf. [62]

Notes

[1] Throughout this section, fundraising is based on the location of the PE firm's advisory team whereas investment and divestment are based on the location of the portfolio company. Fundraising in Sweden

therefore refers to capital raised by funds managed by Swedish PE firms from investors anywhere in the world. Investment and divestment refer to the funding received by and divestments of Swedish companies by any PE fund, regardless of where it is headquartered.

[2] A mutual benefit association is an organisation that provides its members with specific benefits such as financial support for certain types of losses. Instead of paying insurance premiums, members usually contribute through a membership fee, which serves a similar function.

Annex A. Methodology for data collection and classification

Company financial information

Balance sheet information for unlisted non-financial firms

The information on unlisted firms presented in Chapter 2 is based on the OECD-ORBIS Corporate Finance database and includes financial information for non-financial companies between 2005 and 2023.

The raw financial dataset contains multiple firm-year observations due to companies reporting for various purposes. To construct a panel with a single observation per firm-year, the following hierarchical selection criteria are applied:

- Preference is given to financial statements that cover a 12-month period over those with other length.
- For firms with multiple filings in the same year, statements with fiscal year-end dates closest to the calendar year-end (December 31) are prioritised.
- Published annual reports are preferred over local registry filings, which are in turn preferred over filings of unknown type.
- Financials prepared under IFRS are prioritised over those using local GAAP. GAAP-based reports are preferred over those with unspecified accounting standards.
- Where both consolidated and unconsolidated statements are available, consolidated accounts are retained.

Balance sheet information for listed non-financial firms

The information presented in Chapter 2 is based on LSEG Datastream. The unbalanced global panel dataset contains financial statement information for listed non-financial companies between 2000 and 2024. The universe covers 79 418 companies registered in 157 countries. Unless otherwise indicated, the analysis in Chapter 2 is limited to those listed on regulated exchanges and certain major growth markets.

Financial information cleaning

The raw financial dataset contains several firm-year observations when a company reports for different purposes. To construct a panel with a unique firm-year observation, the following steps are applied:

- Financial companies are excluded.
- Security types classified as "trust" are excluded.
- Companies classified as "REITs", "collective investments", "SPACs" and "acquisition corporations" are excluded.
- Financial statements covering a 12-month period are used.
- Observations missing common equity or total liabilities are excluded.

- Year of financial information is adjusted based on the fiscal year of the company.
- Financial information is adjusted by annual US Consumer Price Index changes and information is reported in 2025 USD.
- For companies missing up to 3 years of information, the data is imputed using linear interpolation.

Industry classification

LSEG Datastream uses the Reference data Business Classification (TRBC).

Table A A.1. Industry classifications in the balance sheet data

TRBC Economic Sector	
Basic Materials	Industrials
Cyclical Consumer Goods & Services	Non-Cyclical Consumer Goods & Services
Energy	Real Estate
Financials	Technology
Healthcare	Utilities

Public equity data

The information on initial public offerings (IPOs) and secondary public offerings (SPOs) presented in Chapter 2 is based on transaction and/or firm-level data gathered from several commercial databases (LSEG, FactSet and Bloomberg). Considerable resources have been committed to ensuring the consistency and quality of the dataset. Different data sources are checked against each other and, whenever necessary, the information is also controlled against original sources, including regulatory, stock exchange and company websites as well as financial statements. Industry classifications are those in Table A.1.

Country coverage and classification

The dataset includes information about all IPOs and SPOs by financial and non-financial companies in the period from January 1990 to December 2025.

All public equity listings following an IPO, including first-time listings on an exchange other than the primary exchange, are classified as SPOs. If a company is listed on more than one exchange within 180 days, those transactions are consolidated under one IPO. Unless otherwise indicated, the country breakdown is carried out based on the stock exchange location of the issuer. It is possible that a company becomes listed in more than one country when going public. The financial databases record a dual listing as multiple transactions for each country where the company is listed. However, there is also a significant number of cases where dual listings are reported as one transaction only based on the primary market of the listing. For this reason, the country breakdown based on the stock exchange is currently carried out based on the primary market of the issuer.

Currency conversion and inflation adjustment

The IPO and SPO data, as well as related financial statement data such as total assets before the offering, are collected on a deal-level basis via commercial databases in current USD values. The information is aggregated annually and, in some tables, presented at the year-industry level. Issuance amounts initially collected in USD were adjusted by 2025 US Consumer Price Index (CPI).

Exclusion criteria

The analysis does not consider IPOs and SPOs by trusts, funds and special purpose acquisition companies (SPACs). The following industry categories are therefore excluded:

- Financial companies that conduct trust, fiduciary and custody activities
- Asset management companies such as health and welfare funds, pension funds and their third-party administrators, as well as other financial vehicles
- Open-end investment funds
- Other financial vehicles
- Grant-making foundations
- Asset management companies that deal with trusts, estates and agency accounts
- Special Purpose Acquisition Companies (SPACs)
- Closed-end funds
- Listings on an over-the-counter (OTC) market
- Security types classified as "units" and "trust"
- Real Estate Investment Trusts (REITs)
- Transactions with missing or zero proceeds

Ownership data

The ownership figures for publicly listed companies are based on OECD calculations using firm-level information from the FactSet Ownership database. The data are complemented and verified using LSEG and Bloomberg. Data are collected at the end of 2025 in current USD, thus no inflation adjustment is needed. Market information for each company is collected from LSEG. The dataset includes the records of owners for 43 852 companies listed across 104 countries covering 99% of the world market capitalisation. For each of the countries/regions presented, the information corresponds to all listed companies in those countries/regions with available information.

The records of owners are collected for each company. Some companies have up to 5 000 records in their list of owners. Each record contains the name of the institution, the percentage of outstanding shares owned, the investor type classification, the origin country of the investor, the ultimate parent name, among other things.

Different types of investors are grouped into these five categories of owners. In many cases, when the ultimate owner is identified as a government, a province or a city and the direct owner was not identified as such, ownership records are reclassified as public sector. For example, public pension funds that are regulated under public sector law are classified as public sector, and sovereign wealth funds (SWFs) are also included in that same category.

Table A A.2. Categories of owners defined and used in the report

Investor category	Categories of owners	
	Investor type	
Private corporations and holding companies	Business association	Operating division
	Employee stock ownership plan	Private company
	Holding company	Public company
	Joint venture	Subsidiary
	Non-profit organisation	
Public sector	Government	Regional governments
	Sovereign wealth manager	Public pension funds
Strategic individuals and family members	Individual (Strategic owners)	Family office
Institutional investors	Bank investment division	Mutual fund manager
	Broker	Other
	College/University	Pension fund
	Foundation/Endowment manager	Pension fund manager
	Fund of funds manager	Private banking/Wealth management
	Fund of hedge funds manager	Private equity fund/Alternative investments
	Hedge fund	Real estate manager
	Hedge fund manager	Research firm
	Insurance company	Stock borrowing/Lending
	Investment adviser	Trust/Trustee
	Market maker	Umbrella fund
	Mutual fund-closed end	Venture capital/Private equity
Other free-float including retail investors	Shares in the hands of investors that are not required to disclose their holdings. It includes the direct holdings of retail investors who are not required to disclose their ownership and institutional investors that did not exceed the required thresholds for public disclosure of their holdings.	

Note: Due to ongoing changes in commercial data providers, ownership data may be subject to future revision. Changes are likely to be minor in most regions. Larger differences may be visible in countries with high levels of state ownership.

Private equity data

The main source of information for the private equity data presented in section 2.2 is Invest Europe / EDC. The information provided by Invest Europe comprises firms managing investment vehicles or pools of capital (funds) and primarily investing equity capital in enterprises not quoted on a stock market. Firms are included in the analysis as long as at least one of the funds they manage qualifies; however, only the activity of the qualifying funds is taken into consideration.

The countries included when referring to Europe statistics are: Austria, Baltic countries (Estonia, Latvia, Lithuania), Belgium, Bulgaria, Czechia, Denmark, Finland, France, Germany, Greece, Hungary, Ireland, Italy, Luxembourg, the Netherlands, Norway, Other CEE (Bosnia and Herzegovina, Croatia, Moldova, Montenegro, North Macedonia, Serbia, Slovenia, the Slovak Republic), Poland, Portugal, Romania, Spain, Sweden, Switzerland, Ukraine, and the United Kingdom.

Fundraising activities are classified according to the country that corresponds to the location of the advisory team of the fund. For the CEE region, fundraising activity is the sum of funds managed from the CEE region plus funds that have declared CEE as their target region. The amount reported under investments includes equity, quasi equity, mezzanine, unsecured debt and secured debt. Secured debt amounts within all investment packages are removed, unless the debt originates from private equity funds. Investment activities are recorded according to the location of the portfolio company. Divestment amounts are recorded at cost (i.e. the total amount divested is equal to the total amount invested previously). Private equity statistics are collected in current Euros. Amounts are then adjusted by using Euro CPI to express them in constant 2024 EUR.

The categories of private equity entities that are excluded from the Invest Europe Universe are: Funds of Funds, Hedge Funds, Real Estate, Project Financing/Infrastructure, Secondary Funds, Distressed Debt, Venture Credit, Participative Loans, Incubators, Accelerators, Business Angels and Holding Companies.

Notes on data updates in this report

Figure 2.46: Since the publication of a previous mapping report of the Swedish equity market dating from April 2025 (*The Swedish Equity Market: Institutional Framework and Trends*), historical data on net saving rates in the OECD Economic Outlook have been revised. The figure and the corresponding text commentary have been updated to reflect this change.

www.ingramcontent.com/pod-product-compliance
Lightning Source LLC
LaVergne TN
LVHW060454061126
851857LV00016B/1832
* 9 7 8 9 2 6 4 3 3 5 8 5 1 *